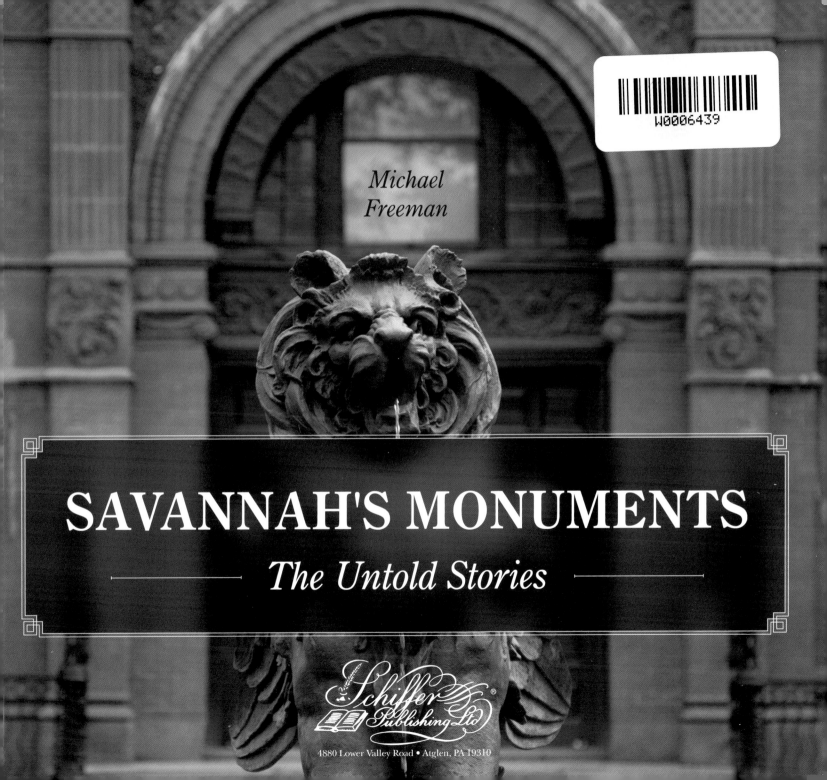

Michael
Freeman

SAVANNAH'S MONUMENTS

The Untold Stories

Schiffer
Publishing Ltd

4880 Lower Valley Road • Atglen, PA 19310

Other Schiffer Books on Related Subjects:

Civil War Walking Tour of Savannah
IDBN: 978-0-7643-2537-3

Savannah Squares
ISBN: 978-0-7643-2047-7

Art in Savannah
ISBN: 978-0-7643-2649-3

Designed by Justin Watkinson Cover by Molly Shields
Type set in CenturyOldst BT/Minion Pro

ISBN: 978-0-7643-4903-4
Printed in China

Published by Schiffer Publishing, Ltd.
4880 Lower Valley Road
Atglen, PA 19310
Phone: (610) 593-1777; Fax: (610) 593-2002
E-mail: Info@schifferbooks.com

For our complete selection of fine books on this and related subjects,
please visit our website at www.schifferbooks.com. You may also write for a free catalog.

This book may be purchased from the publisher. Please try your bookstore first.

We are always looking for people to write books on new and related subjects.
If you have an idea for a book, please contact us at proposals@schifferbooks.com.

Schiffer Publishing's titles are available at special discounts for bulk purchases for sales promotions or premiums. Special editions, including personalized covers, corporate imprints, and excerpts can be created in large quantities for special needs. For more information, contact the publisher.

ACKNOWLEDGMENTS

I thank my fellow citizens and those who have gone before us for their part in creating this city.

I am also fortunate to stand on the shoulders of many historians: professional and amateur, present and past, who have helped us in our ongoing discovery of Savannah. No one is an island. So I thank all of those who have researched and offered insight into my understanding of Savannah's history over the years. I wish to thank the Roads Scholar Program at Armstrong Atlantic State University in allowing me to present my findings to these visitors of Savannah. It has helped me to identify the interest and information people need and want in order to understand and appreciate our city's monuments.

I wish to offer my great appreciation of Chris Ford, who at the last minute gave me valuable technical assistance. And of course a thank you to Schiffer's editor Dinah Roseberry whose work, advice, and prompt responses made the project so much easier.

On a personal note, I wish to thank my parents, Tom and Katherine, for creating in me an interest and love of the world about me. Thanks to my children Maya, Dorothy (thanks for taking the Toomer monument photographs), and Philip, who keep the old man on his toes by making him see the world through different eyes. And as always thank you to my wife, Dr. Christine Neal—she has been a superb editor, has served as advisor, and has made life and writing easier and more fun.

CONTENTS

PREFACE

This book came out of my interest in the history of, and my love for, the city of Savannah, which continues to be one of the most beautiful and interesting places in the world.

It is said that in the nineteenth century, Baltimore was known as the city of monuments. Savannah leaders of that century wanted to rival—if not take—the title away from Baltimore and, thus, began an era of monument-making that continues to this day.

Monuments can tell you a lot about a people: what they cherish, the point of view they want to communicate to the world, and the scope of their concerns. We are proud of our history and desire to tell it to all who visit, as well as to our future generations. But, with each piece of story told, there lies another story beneath the surface. Savannah has wonderful tales to tell her children, but there are also stories the adults tell when their children are asleep, tucked in their beds. The story I wish to tell is the proud history we repeat to our children, as well as those things that we wish to tell them when they come of age.

In the past, monuments recorded *accepted* history. The history they wish to tell is the history of the majority or those who are—or were—in power. In early times, rulers made monuments to commemorate their great battles and accomplishments, yet mention nothing of the people they conquered. As the continual democratization of public space takes place, we see glimmers of other histories being told. This book is designed to act as a history lesson, reflecting on who we are as a city's people and our place in that public history.

The oldest city in Georgia and the thirteenth colony; she has plenty of history to offer. For centuries, that history primarily reflected the white-male experience; but, in more recent times, there have been monuments to the African-American experience. Yet, still, women with historic significance are not represented in equal measure to their contributions, and Native Americans are literally pushed to one side. The community is involved, as well, and the processes of constructing monuments also reflect the ongoing struggles of individual neighborhoods.

This book is written to capture the imagination and ongoing storytelling of Savannah through her monuments. The book includes topics that discuss: how much should be said about slavery and the Middle Passage, whether monuments should be constructed on hallowed graves, who the designers of monuments are or should be in the future, the memorializing of confederate history, whether "touristory" should be more important than history, and many other themes.

I will leave to you decide whether Savannah has succeeded in her quest to become known as the city of monuments.

I

AVENUE OF HEROES

THE
BULL STREET
MONUMENTS

If there is a most treasured road in Savannah, it is Bull Street—a road that, if we started at the south end of Forsyth Park and walked all the way to the place of Savannah's European beginnings, River Street, we would encounter what I call the Avenue of Heroes. Forsyth Park has three monuments and each square north along Bull Street has at least one major monument to a hero or important event. Most of these monuments were designed by the greatest sculptors of their day. When we at last reach River Street, we can experience the heart of the city. Businesses, tourists, and huge cargo ships are present, along with an eclectic range of monuments commemorating a local legend, the Olympics; a steamship; the African-American family; and a World War II Memorial.

Savannah has a multitude of stories to tell. If you walk among her trees and squares, along her river, visit her monuments, and see her museums, you would know that she is a city with mysteries—as well as new legends that are unfolding all the time. Her story is neither simple nor complex. It is human.

British Evacuation:
The Lost Monument

The Lost Monument marker once held a prominent place in Savannah. It stood where the *Georgia Volunteer* sculpture (examined later) stands today, at the southern end of Forsyth Park. In 1904, the Lachlan McIntosh Chapter, Daughters of the American Revolution of Savannah, proposed to commemorate Evacuation Day here, every year on July 11. Evacuation Day marked the day, in 1782, the British and their Loyalist allies left the city after its occupation during the Revolutionary War. The Chapter selected a bronze drinking fountain as an appropriate monument.

Mayor Herman Myers, the leader in the construction of City Hall, accepted the monument on behalf of Savannah. The concept was that the monument would anchor the end of Bull Street.[1] At the north end of the street would be City Hall; in between were the squares and their prominent monuments. Forsyth Park with the fountain was on its north end. The best laid plans of mice and men, however, do not always work. The fountain was hit by a wagon and destroyed beyond repair. Over the years, other Savannah monuments have been the victims of cars. The Cotton Exchange Lion and the Armillary in Troup Square both were severely damaged by automobiles and later repaired. This spot lay bare until the *Georgia Volunteer* monument was placed there.

Evacuation Day is one of the more important moments in Savannah's history. After four years of occupation,

The remaining plaque for the Lost Monument. The *Georgia Volunteer* in the background is where the Lost Monument once stood.

the British left Savannah, seven months after the surrender of Yorktown that ended the Revolutionary War. Governor Wright, the royal provincial governor, had been thrown out of office and forced into exile. Two years later, Wright came back from England after British troops recaptured the city in the First Battle for Savannah. Despite another bloody battle for Savannah, the city had stayed in English hands until 1782.

Savannah was one of three ports from which the British evacuated; the other two were Charleston and New York. The 1,200 British soldiers at the garrison in Savannah, along with Loyalists, boarded ships and sailed out of the city on Evacuation Day. Meanwhile, General Nathaniel Greene was afraid that these departing troops would land in Charleston where the combined numbers of British troops would be greater than his forces. So General Greene commanded General Anthony Wayne to take his troops from the Savannah area to Charleston. General Wayne, however, had one more battle to fight just outside of Savannah on Skidaway Island.[2] The British soldiers were intermittently attacking coastal islands as they evacuated to gain supplies and slaves. One such effort was on Skidaway Island where General Wayne and his Lieutenant Colonel James Jackson ordered their forces to engage the British, effectively forcing them to abandon the Georgia coast. This is said to be the last Revolutionary battle in Georgia.

This marker is often overlooked; it is not listed in Savannah's catalogue of monuments and markers. The story is one of a monument lost and an

The plaque that once stood at the fountain of the Lost Monument.

example of what would happen if we were to lose the memorials we have. For this story, a day once celebrated is gone; no one knows very much about Evacuation Day today. The reminder of how we once were occupied with our patriots captured or having to flee is only seldom mentioned in textbooks. Where would we be as a country if the Lincoln Memorial was to disappear? Or if the Vietnam Wall was not there to help people remember the lives of those lost in a war many feel was not needed. Likewise, here in Savannah what if the *Waving Girl* was never constructed? Or if the Haitian Monument did not stand to tell of their contribution to

our freedom? I believe that by losing monuments, we lose part of ourselves as a people in a proud city—our story not whole. This Lost Monument is a testimony to how quickly they can be destroyed or lost and that care must be taken to ensure that their history and what they represent are not forgotten.

Spanish-American War Monument: Am I Prolific or What?

The Spanish-American War was ready-made to unite a nation that, after the Civil War, was still very much divided by sectionalism. Theodore Roosevelt,

The Spanish American Monument faces south toward Cuba at the southern entrance of Forsyth Park. Forsyth Park was used as a training field for Spanish American soldiers.

as leader of the Rough Riders who would become one of the heroes of the war, wrote in his memoir, "Everywhere we saw the Stars and Stripes, and everywhere we were told, half-laughing, by grizzled ex-Confederates that they had never dreamed in the bygone days of bitterness to greet the old flag as they now were greeting it, and to send their sons, as now they were sending them, to fight and die under it."[3]

The War would revive our expansionist ideals. We had secured and expanded our country from sea to shining sea; where were we to go next? Canada, as some had suggested, was one answer, but the events leading to the Spanish-American War led our wayward eyes to Spanish territories. The War revived a nationalism in 1898, thirty-three years after the Civil War. One of the many reasons it resurrected nationalism was that the war was short, lasting less than ten weeks. Another was the general dislike of Spain in America. The Spaniards did not want Cuban independence from their empire. America favored the Cuban Independence movement and we were very leery of a European power having a foothold so close to us.

Our entry into the war was brought on by the mysterious sinking of an American ship called the *Maine* which was docked at the port of Havana, Cuba. This sinking gave the United States a good battle cry: "Remember the *Maine*," and a just cause (Cuban independence). This cause shows weakening by most current historians, who now conclude the *Maine* was not attacked but exploded due to a mechanical failure. Finally, the end result was that we not only won, but acquired more land: Puerto Rico, Guam, and the Philippines. Even in the South, these things created a feel good about America.

In Savannah, 13,000 troops from across Georgia came to the newly christened Camp Onward. These soldiers ranged in encampment from the town of Thunderbolt down Victory Drive to Forsyth Park. Savannah was selected as the point of embarkation for the Seventh Army Corps, commanded by General Fitzhugh Lee. Lee was the nephew of Robert E. Lee and a lieutenant in the Confederacy. Before shipping out for occupation duty in Cuba or Puerto Rico, the men of Camp Onward held a grand review on December 17, 1898, for President McKinley and Generals Lawton, Shafter, and Wheeler. A large banquet was then held at the old Desoto Hotel for the corps' officers and visiting dignitaries. You might have noticed that these troops were headed for occupation duty, not battle. By the time most soldiers were recruited, shipped to training camps, trained, and ready for battle, the war was over. Only 379 soldiers died in actual combat. More would die of various tropical diseases than battle wounds.

At the south end of Forsyth Park stands a monument called the *Georgia Volunteer*. It is a monument in honor of the veterans of the Spanish-American War. The base of the monument was designed by Savannah architect Cletus Bergen. In the twentieth century, Bergen and his father designed homes and offices, apartments and churches, military buildings and mansions. Some of their work may be seen in St. Paul's Greek Orthodox Church, Drayton Tower, St. Mary's Home, Savannah State University's library, and many of the city's Tudor-style homes.

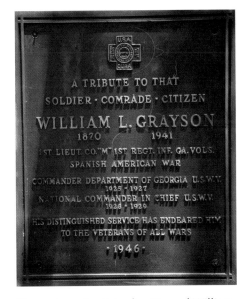

Plaque honoring Brigadier General William Grayson, Savannah's Spanish American hero.

The following words can be found on the west face of the base of the monument:

A tribute to that
Soldier · Comrade · Citizen
William L. Grayson
1870   1941
1st. Lieut. Co. "M" 1st Regt. Ga. Vols.
Spanish-American War
Commander Department of Georgia U.S.W.V.

William L. Grayson was a significant Savannah civic leader during his life. He served as the first chief of the Fire Commission. After a hurricane destroyed what was then called Municipal Field, he was the civic leader in charge of raising 150,000 dollars to reconstruct what is now called Grayson Stadium in Daffin Park. This stadium is where the Class A Sand Gnats baseball team plays and where such baseball greats as Babe Ruth, Mickey Mantle, Jackie Robinson, and Hank Aaron have played.

Grayson's name is prominent on the memorial because he was the first Southerner to serve as commander of the United States War Veterans of the Spanish-American War. He served only a short term in active field service because of the brevity of the war.

The statue on top of the base is one of the three sculptures by women found in the Historic District of Savannah. Women sculptors were hard to find in the nineteenth- and early-twentieth centuries. Theo Alice Ruggles was one of the few recognized. At the age of fourteen, she made a snow sculpture in the yard of her family's Brookline, Massachusetts, home. This was no ordinary snowman. It showed a recumbent horse in the act of rising from the ground, and it attracted notice in the neighborhood and beyond. People from Boston were said to make the trip out to Brookline just to see it.

Her parents, realizing they had a prodigy, tried unsuccessfully to enroll her in an art school. Art schools were usually a male domain and women were not allowed. After an extensive search, they found a young British sculptor, Henry Hudson Kitson, who was willing to take her on as a student. It marked the beginning of a journey that would lead, in just a few years, to the Paris Salon and a partnership and marriage to Kitson, as well as to the recognition of her as one of the most accomplished American sculptors in her day.

Henry Hudson Kitson was twenty years old when he began working with Ruggles. He took her to Paris to further her studies. (Do not worry: to make everything proper, her mother joined them.) In 1888, Ruggles had one of her sculptures accepted in the Paris Salon. It was called *The Shepherd Lad* and was highly praised. But the sculpture was listed under the name Mr. Theo Ruggles, perhaps to ensure she had a fair review. It was a practice of some up-and-coming women artists to use a male name to assure a fair hearing and not receive a dismissal of her work merely based on her gender. Whatever the case, the following year, while still a teenager, she became the first American woman sculptor to receive an award—honorable mention—at the Salon for her work entitled *Orpheus*.

Ruggles succeeded, despite the barriers women of her day faced. Women artists were expected to paint flowers and other domestic subjects. They were not allowed to have nude models because of the supposed impropriety, but also because, it was thought, they were simply incapable of rendering the human form satisfactorily.

Lorado Taft, an art critic, praised one of her works, applauding the power and strength of it, but then added, "One is almost compelled to qualify the somewhat sweeping assertion that no woman has, as yet, modeled the male figure to look like a man."[4] Camille Claudel, a contemporary woman artist of Kitson success, was described this way by art critic Octave Mirbeau: she was "a revolt against nature: a woman genius."[5]

Close-up of the *Georgia Volunteer*.

Perhaps most remarkably for a woman in that era, Theo Ruggles Kitson became one of the leading sculptors of war memorials in the United States, with statues, busts, and reliefs on display from coast to coast commemorating the Civil War, the Spanish-American War, and World War I.

But probably her most viewed work is *The Hiker* or, as we call it here in Savannah, the *Georgia Volunteer*, the monument now found on the south end of Forsyth Park. There are fifty-two of these monuments across America. It may be the most prolific statue in the United States. It can be found

Side view of the *Georgia Volunteer,* one of the most prolific monuments in the United States.

in New Orleans, Louisiana; Arcadia County, California; Arlington National Cemetery, Washington, DC; Austin, Texas; St. Paul, Minnesota; and many other cities. The monument has become representative of the Spanish-American War. It is so uniquely spread across the US, and because the bronze for each statue is mixed in the same way for each memorial, it allows the statue to be used to compare the effects of acid rain for different parts of the country. The proliferation of this monument, representing the volunteer soldiers of the Spanish-American War, alludes to a newfound unity that the war brought to America. The scars of the Civil War, while not gone, were healing and would only be opened in new, major crises.[6]

Confederate Monument: Yankee Hands Stay Off My Monument

The South was hurting after the Civil War. The economy was wrecked, a way of life was gone, and the land was war-scarred, especially by Sherman's March. The Lost Cause was here, but even worse than all of these things was the grief. At least 250,000 soldiers of the Southern Army had been killed in the war. Many of these dead were in unmarked graves or left rotting on battlefields. Southerners did not always have the means to appropriately retrieve their loved ones' bodies and give them respectful burials. So they grieved. The North, too, grieved, but they had the victorious government trying to assure their dead were respectfully treated. They declared a national day of remembrance, Memorial Day, which

was for the Union soldiers only. By 1870, the remains of nearly 300,000 Union dead had been buried in seventy-three national cemeteries, located mostly in the South, near the battlefields where they died.

Arlington Cemetery, the most prestigious and well known of the national cemeteries, was created to bury the Union dead. General Meigs, a native of Georgia, recommended that the property in Virginia, owned by Mary Custis Lee, the wife of Robert E. Lee, be used as a military burial ground. Meigs was formerly under the command of Lee before the war, making one wonder if there were a personal vendetta. Even if it was not personal, to some Southerners, it appeared a vindictive move by the North.[6]

The Arlington House, once associated with George Washington and the founding of the nation, had taken on a new context—one of defiance—and was associated with the leader of the Confederate Army, Robert E. Lee. Many Northerners felt that the building would never be associated with Washington, but now his legacy would be overshadowed by Lee. This was intolerable. So the land that surrounded the house was transformed to a cemetery to honor the heroic Union soldiers. The first soldiers were buried there in mid-May, 1864.[7]

Although Confederate soldiers *were* buried at Arlington, their families were prevented from decorating their graves or even visiting the cemetery because it was considered a Union burial ground. When, in 1868, a group of Southern women asked to place flowers at the

The Confederate Monument sits in the center of Savannah's Forsyth Park.

Confederate graves, "they were curtly refused" entry to the grounds.[8] General John A. Logan of the Grand Army of the Republic ordered that the rebels' graves be specifically ignored by the hundreds of volunteers who decorated Union graves.

A Confederate memorial and burial ground in Arlington Cemetery would not be approved by Congress until 1900. In 1914, the thirty-two-foot-tall sculpture honoring the Confederate dead was unveiled by President Woodrow Wilson (a Southerner and married to the daughter of the minister of Savannah's Independent Presbyterian Church). This was made possible by several factors: the country returned to economic normalcy, conditions allowed room for public and privately-funded memorials, the Spanish-American War had given the two sides a common cause again, and most of the great heroes of the Civil War began to die off. Beginning with Robert E. Lee in 1870, most of the other high command from both sides were dead by 1890.

Arlington was not the only place the Confederate dead were not honored. News from one Richmond article reported on conditions in Petersburg, Virginia. The bodies of dead Confederate soldiers laying in the fields and not interred were so numerous, the farmers could not cultivate the soil. In Shiloh and Corinth, 12,000 Confederate dead lay on the fields, while the Federal dead were neatly interred with head and footbounds, reported the *Savannah Daily Herald*.

The South would respond to the non-inclusion of their soldiers in Memorial Day events and national cemeteries. Beginning in 1866, the Southern states had their own Memorial Days, ranging from April 26 to mid-June. The birthday of Confederate President Jefferson Davis, June 3rd, became a state holiday in ten states by 1916. Across the South, associations were founded after the War to establish and care for permanent cemeteries for Confederate soldiers, organize commemorative ceremonies, and sponsor impressive monuments as a permanent way of remembering the Confederate tradition.

In Savannah, the veterans of the Confederacy formed an association. Later, as the veterans died off, the Sons of the Confederacy would be founded to carry on the traditions. Women were usually found doing most of the work in auxiliary committees to the various Confederate groups that were formed. This paved the way for women to establish themselves as capable of public leadership—because of so many male deaths in the War, a vacuum in leadership existed that they were able to fill.

The War and the divide over the treatment and honor of the dead would continue a regionalist rivalry that can still be seen today. In Georgia, there were three national cemeteries for Union soldiers in the works. Out of bitterness and great pain, the women of Savannah would respond. Usually, the victors write the history and make the monuments, but these steely magnolias would change that. In 1892, the Confederate Veterans' Association of Savannah issued a call to the ladies of the city to form an auxiliary to their organization. This group became the Ladies Memorial Association; they would serve for thirty years, between 1867 and 1897. Savannah had 500 uncared-for graves of Confederate soldiers.

Mrs. Anna Mitchell Davenport (Raines) was one of the ladies who responded. She (along with the other ladies in the group) began to protect and preserve a Southern soldier cemetery at Savannah's prestigious Laurel Grove Cemetery. It was modeled after the national cemeteries being created for the Union soldiers—only they flew a Confederate flag to designate the site. The South's economy was wrecked, but these ladies, with determination, decided they would cajole the leaders of the community to help them in the plan. This cemetery can still be found within historical Laurel Grove Cemetery. The women also decided to go one step further: they would create a monument to memorialize the Confederate dead. This would become, if not the first, one of the first, Confederate monuments in the South. These two endeavors would keep them busy for several years. But Mrs. Raines had an even greater vision of what Southern women could do to preserve the memories of Confederate dead.

Anna Mitchell Davenport (Raines) was born on April 8, 1853, at Isle of Hope, Savannah, Georgia. Her parents were Major Hugh McCall Davenport and Martha Anne Elizabeth Stone. She was the granddaughter of Isaiah Davenport, a shipbuilder, whose home's preservation became the impetus for the founding of the Historic Savannah Foundation. A child when the War began, at the age of ten she was taking food and bandages to the Confederate hospitals and soldiers' camps in Savannah.

Anna was a strong leader and was elected secretary of the Ladies Auxiliary. She soon realized that, as an auxiliary to the veterans, their reason for existence would pass away with the death of those veterans; she suggested at the December 1893 Auxiliary meeting that they form themselves into a permanent organization with wider aims and scope and change their name to "Daughters of the Confederacy." The suggestion met with the approval of the members and she was empowered to secure a charter. This was done and Mrs. Raines was elected the first president.

At the time, she was unaware that there was another society bearing the name "Daughters of the Confederacy." A few weeks later, she saw an article in the newspaper giving an account of a dinner that had been served at the Soldiers' Home in Nashville, Tennessee, by the Daughters of the Confederacy. On April 18, 1894, she wrote a letter to ask whether the Savannah Auxiliary could use this name or would this be an infringement upon their rights. Not knowing whom to write, she addressed her letter to "The President, Daughters of the Confederacy." It was Caroline Meriwether Goodlett who replied to her letter, stating that they were simply organized as an auxiliary to their Soldiers' Home. This correspondence began a women's organization devoted to the Southern ideals and respect and pride in their Southern ancestry.

At the Second Annual Convention held in Atlanta, Georgia, in November of 1895, the name of the organization was decided to be "United Daughters of the Confederacy." Mrs. John C. Brown of Nashville, though not present, was elected president and Mrs. Raines was elected first vice president. On May 12, 1896, Mrs. Brown resigned as president and Mrs. Raines assumed the presidency. Immediately after Mrs. Brown's resignation, Mrs. Isabella M. Clarke, the secretary, left for a trip to Europe leaving Mrs. Raines to hold the three offices for the remainder of the year.

Mrs. Raines's words at the Third Annual Convention in Nashville showed the conservative Southern belle she was, "Let me thank you for your patience and ask in all the discussions that may arise, you will ever keep the holiness of our work before you, remembering we are not a body of discontented suffragists thirsting for oratorical honors, but a sisterhood of earnest womanly women, striving to fulfill the teachings of God's word, in honoring our fathers."[9] Mrs. Raines died on January 21, 1915. She is buried in her family plot in Laurel Grove Cemetery, Savannah, Georgia.

The Savannah Confederate Monument project was begun in 1867, when the Ladies Memorial Association of Savannah, which Mrs. Raines had been instrumental in founding and which was a precursor to the United Daughters of the Confederacy, started raising funds for a memorial for the Confederate dead.

Legend has it that the ladies did not want any Yankee hands to work on the monument. Although I cannot find any reference by the women of this desire, I can say, unlike other monuments in Savannah that had renowned sculptors from Boston, New York, and Philadelphia, they chose Robert Reid, a Scot, whose studio was in Nova Scotia. The monument is made of Nova Scotia sandstone and was shipped by a British schooner from Halifax, not touching land until it reached Savannah. The monument, upon entry, was seized by the US Customs House because the British captain was in violation of US customs regulations. They had no money for the unexpected customs fee. Colonel Atkins of US Customs, wisely realizing the hornet's nest he was in, quickly gave the women of Savannah a free pass on the import fees and penalties.

When the monument was finally unveiled, it shocked the sensibilities of the Savannah women. It was a monument filled with allegories and Victorian ornamental style. While this style was the up-and-coming fashion for monuments, one can imagine the confusion and raised eyebrows of conservative women, such as Mrs. Raines. They had conceived in their heads a realistic, proud-but-simple monument. What they got were marble figures at the middle and the top of the monument, representing Judgment and Silence/Death, and Victorian gingerbread carved cornices and columns. A close look at Reid's existing work may have prepared the ladies for what his work was like, because a previous work in Toronto called the *Canadian Volunteer* was similar. As far as they were concerned, it was a disaster of sensibilities.

Close-up of the bottom of the Confederate Monument. Notice the Victorian embellishments that Savannah's Ladies Memorial Association disliked.

It was at this point that George Wimberly Jones Derenne, local businessman and grandson of Noble Jones, one of the original colonists, came to the ladies' aid. He pledged to the women to "fix" the monument at his own expense. But he would do so only if they gave him control of the project. The ladies, who were more than grateful, agreed to his demand and he began to "fix" the monument. His efforts would soon redeem the project.

The statue of Judgment was donated to Thomasville, Georgia, for its own monument and the marble statue of Silence/Death was carted off to

Confederate cemetery in Savannah's historic Laurel Grove Cemetery. The statue of "Silence" removed from the Confederate Monument stands in the background.

Close-up of the "Silence" statue.

Savannah's Laurel Grove Cemetery to watch over the Confederate burial ground the Savannah chapter of the United Daughters of the Confederacy had established.

The next thing he did would have been controversial, if the legend about the women not wanting Yankee hands on the project were true. He acquired the services of sculptor David Richard, a Welshman from (heaven forbid) Utica, New York, to sculpt the Confederate soldier atop the memorial. Yankee hands were now on the monument!

Yet the statue was a realistic figure with which the women would have been comfortable. But maybe it was the fine words, his lineage, and the fact he was footing the bill that Mr. Derenne was able to assuage any reluctance to allow Yankee hands on the memorial. In a speech before the Association he said "....the statue represents the soldier as he was.... marked with the marks of service in features, form, and nascent, a man who chose rather to be seen, to bear hardship, then to complain of it, a man who met with unflinching firmness the fate decreed to him to suffer, to fight, and to die in vain. A tribute to the men of the Confederacy without name, or face, or hope of gain they did their duty appointed of them."

Every year, the Sons and Daughters of the Confederacy hold a service at the monument in remembrance of the Confederate dead. No stranger sight could have been seen than when the first African-American mayor of Savannah, in May of 1998, stood before the monument and took part in the service. The crowd of about 250 who assembled for the ceremony ranged from curious tourists with cameras to matrons in flower-print dresses and straw hats waving Confederate battle flags.

"Our armies did not give us victory in the war, but something more powerful and enduring: our heritage," said Jennie Zuccarini, president of the Savannah chapter of the United Daughters of the Confederacy. Alongside reenactors in Confederate uniforms were women dressed in antebellum gowns and carrying parasols—including a woman

Confederate soldier stands aloft at the monument acting as a sentinel for the Lost Cause.

in black with a veil covering her face, representing a war widow.

Blaine Jenkins, commander of Savannah's Sons of Confederate Veterans chapter, echoed the day's theme of Southern pride. "Heritage is our blood-born right," he said. "There's no shame in being Southern. We have the greatest nation, being Americans, and the greatest heritage, being Southerners."

Mayor Floyd Adams Jr., Savannah's first African-American mayor, made his third appearance in three years at the observance, saying that everyone should be proud of their heritage. "We must all work together, regardless of what ethnicity we are," said Adams, who was greeted with cheers by the uniformed Civil War reenactors. "We are one America, one Georgia and—most of all—we are one Savannah."[10] "Racial unity" was the theme of Mayor Adams' term in office. Many thought he did not do enough for the black community and concentrated on the white business community too much. Savannah's second African-American mayor did not feel the need to attend the services.

Out of their pain and grief, the women of Savannah's yesteryears have erected a monument that has stood for over 135 years. Their loved ones and friends have not been forgotten. The weary soldier atop the memorial looks north, where once a foe came, but now only memories of a lost cause exist. The observances continue as a part of who Savannah was and is.

Savannah has played a major part in keeping the memories of the Confederate dead alive. But Savannah has not idealized the antebellum period and the Civil War as their rival sister city, Charleston, and other cities have. Just as their soldiers rest from battle, life in Savannah continues on proudly, as she proclaims other parts of herself: the Revolutionary War, economic successes, historic city planning, an active port city, the arts, and other facets.

Today, Savannah lives and thrives with a people busy creating their own history and millions of tourists coming to see her. But always underneath the bustling activity, there is the faint echo of a tragic war.

Bartow and McLaws Busts: Heroes of the Lost Cause

Enclosed in the fence with the Confederate Monument are two busts of Savannah Confederate heroes. These busts originally were in Chippewa Square, but when the city commissioned the Oglethorpe Monument for the Square, the Confederate heroes were moved to their present location.

On the south side is Colonel Francis S. Bartow; he was the first prominent Georgian to be killed in the Civil War. His death would bring home the coming tragedy of so many promising lives that would be lost. He was a skilled lawyer, served two terms as representative, and one term as senator in the Georgia Assembly. He was also involved in the forming of the Confederacy and was a strong influence on the vote for Georgia to secede from the Union. He was even responsible for the color and style of the Confederate Uniform, insisting the gray uniform of the Savannah Volunteer Guard be adopted.[11]

As the elected captain of Savannah's Oglethorpe Light Infantry, he was in charge of capturing Fort Pulaski at the mouth of the Savannah River at the beginning of the Civil War. At the First Battle of Manassas, on July 21, 1861, during a critical moment, he seized the regimental colors and attempted to lead a charge on a Union battery, but he was shot through the heart. He died with his last words being, "They have killed me boys, but never give up the field."[12]

FRANCIS S. BARTOW
COLONEL 8TH. REGT.
GEORGIA VOLUNTEERS
CONFEDERATE STATES ARMY
BORN SAVANNAH Ca.
SEPTEMBER 6TH. 1816.
FELL AT MANASSAS
JULY 21ST. 1861.

Bust of Francis Bartow, the first prominent Savannahian to die in the Civil War. The monument sits on the south side of the Confederate Monument.

LAFAYETTE McLAWS
MAJOR GENERAL
CONFEDERATE STATES ARMY
BORN AUGUSTA Ca.
JANUARY 15TH. 1821.
DIED SAVANNAH Ca.
JULY 24TH. 1897.

Bust of Lafayette McLaws, another Savannah Confederate hero. The monument sits on the north side of the Confederate Monument.

Bartow's body was returned to Savannah and buried in the family plot at Laurel Grove Cemetery.

The other bust is of Lafayette McLaws, an officer in the United States Army. When the Civil War commenced, he resigned and joined the Confederate Army.

He was made a major general and fought with General James Longstreet. His leadership was questioned by Longstreet when McLaws' troops were slow to come to his aid at the battle of Fort Sanders in Tennessee. Longstreet, angry and questioning the abilities of McLaws, relieved him of his command. The Confederate War Department, in what some believed was a political move, reinstated him over Longstreet's objections. Yet, realizing he could no longer serve with Longstreet, he was moved to the Georgia field of action and served under General Joseph Johnston.

After the War, McLaws served as Savannah's postmaster from 1875 to 1876, and was active in Savannah's Confederate veterans' organizations.

Lafayette McLaws died in Savannah and is buried at Laurel Grove Cemetery.

The busts were created by the Romanian-born George Julian Zolnay, known as "the Sculptor of the Confederacy." Zolnay also produced busts of Confederate spy Sam Davis and the Soldiers' Monument, both in Nashville, Tennessee. He sculpted Confederate President Jefferson Davis for Davis' grave in Richmond at Hollywood Cemetery.

The two Savannah Civil War hero busts tell different stories. The one reminds us of the tragedy of a life lost so young and the other of a man who overcame early mistakes and fears to reclaim his honor.

Forsyth Park Fountain: We Love the French

Forsyth Park was the first large park created in Savannah. The park was created in the 1840s on land donated by William Hodgson. In 1851, the park was expanded and named for Georgia Governor John Forsyth. It now comprises thirty acres. The Park was influenced by all things French. In Paris, an urban renewal movement was afoot, where broad boulevards and parks were the fashion.

The 1850s were a prosperous period throughout the South and the high style of the French Empire was admired and emulated in everything from wallpaper to furniture, architecture, and as shown in the photo, city design.

The Forsyth Park Fountain was thought to be a copy of the one in the Place de la Concorde by Jacques Ignace Hittorff, who completed two monumental fountains in that plaza only a few short years before Forsyth Park was created. Bull Street was thought of as a boulevard and promenade (both French terms) and the Fountain served as a focal point of a long vista to City Hall.

Forsyth Fountain in all its splendor.

Copies of this fountain can be found in three other places: Poughkeepsie, New York; Madison, Indiana; and Cuzco, Peru.

The Fountain has undergone some changes through the years. During the installation of the Forsyth Fountain, in 1858, the pool was enlarged and the fixtures rearranged because of the high water pressure that caused the water to spout too vigorously. In 1988, the Fountain was completely restored by Robinson Iron Works of Alexander City, Alabama, financed in part by the city and private donations, much of which came from the sale of "signature bricks" at the base of the fountain. For this restoration, the Georgia Trust for Historic Preservation gave the Park

Detail of the top of Forsyth Fountain.

Forsyth Fountain sits at the north end of Forsyth Park. It is approached by a wide boulevard with oak trees lining both sides.

and Tree Commission an award for an "Outstanding Restoration."

Today, the Fountain is one of the most photographed subjects in Savannah; it has become an iconic symbol of our city.

Marine Corps Monument: From the Halls of Montezuma

Across the Savannah River, in Port Royal, South Carolina, resides the Marine Corps Recruit Depot, Parris Island, an 8,095-acre military installation. Male recruits living east of the Mississippi River and female recruits from all over the United States report here to receive their initial training. Noted writer Pat Conroy sets his classic book *The Great Santini* at the Navy/Marine airfield there.

So, it is no surprise that on Armistice Day, November 11, 1947, a memorial to the twenty-four United States Marines from Chatham County killed in World War II, was erected at Bull and Gaston Streets, at the entrance to Forsyth Park. Later, plaques added the names of Marines from Chatham County killed in the Korean and Vietnam Wars.

Bronze plaques and the emblem of the United States Marines, earth, anchor, and eagle, are attached to one large piece of white Georgia marble, four feet, three inches high, three feet, eight inches wide and eight feet long, in a low, simple, rectangular shape, resting on a larger base of similar stone. The design was made to be compatible with Forsyth Fountain.

Today, the monument stands at the north end of the park, reminding us the Marine Corps stands ever faithful.

Marine Memorial as approached from the north side.

Marine Memorial as approached from the south side.

Pulaski Monument: Father of the American Cavalry

Chicago bills itself as having the largest Polish population outside of Warsaw. The Poles are the third largest ethnic group in Illinois, and every first Monday in March, since 1977, Chicago has celebrated Pulaski Day. City schools, libraries, and government offices are closed for the day. This is a holiday with a parade to celebrate the Polish hero Casimir Pulaski. Meanwhile, Georgia rates forty-first in the United States in its Polish population and, yet, Savannah, Georgia's oldest city, has a towering monument in honor of Pulaski, too.

General Count Casimir Pulaski was memorialized for his loyalty to the cause of liberty during the American Revolutionary War. He was born in Lithuania and began his military career by rebelling against Stanislaw II, the

Lady Liberty sits atop Pulaski Monument. The cornice at her feet started falling in the 1990s, causing a $1.5 million dollar restoration.

last King of Poland. For his actions, he was condemned to death, so he escaped Poland and made his way to Paris.

In Paris, he met and was recruited by Benjamin Franklin to join the American cause of liberty; he quickly joined with Washington's forces. Washington was constantly approached by foreigners who wished to assist him in his efforts, if he would merely give them troops to lead. In a letter to Washington, Pulaski wrote, "I come here where freedom is being defended, to serve it, and to live or die for it."[13]

At the Battle of Brandywine, Pulaski showed his courage as he led a cavalry charge at the British forces trying to capture Washington's fleeing army. His maneuvers and gallantry allowed the retreating Washington cover. (As I always say, if you want a promotion at your job, saving your boss's life will help.) The appreciative Washington commissioned Pulaski as a brigadier-general. Pulaski, an expert in cavalry battle, organized and trained his legion of horsemen. He fought with General Washington in Germantown before he went south and fought in the battle for Charleston. The efforts of Pulaski in creating and training the colonists' cavalry would lead to him being called the father of the American cavalry.

It was in the Battle of Savannah that General Pulaski, in an effort to rally the retreating troops, charged the redoubt and was mortally wounded on October 9, 1779. The Battle of Savannah would be lost by the colonists and become one of the bloodiest in the Revolutionary War. The wounded Pulaski was recovered

and taken to a ship called the *Wasp,* off the bluff of Thunderbolt, where he died. Pulaski would become one of only seven people in the United States history to be awarded honorary citizenship.

In the beginning, the monument that now sits in Johnson Square dedicated to General Nathaniel Greene, served as a memorial for both Greene and Pulaski. The obelisk, in part, was left uninscribed until 1886, because city leaders planned to build a monument to Pulaski later. But cities across the nation were holding ceremonies and building monuments to the founders of our nation in response to a visit from the Marquis de Lafayette designed to reinvigorate national pride. The cornerstone for the proposed Pulaski/Greene monument was laid in Chippewa Square, by Lafayette, during his visit to Savannah in 1825. By 1852, enough additional money had been raised by the citizens of Savannah to erect a monument to Pulaski.

They chose renowned Polish sculptor Robert Launitz and gave him the power to choose an appropriate site—instead of the suggested Chippewa Square, he chose Monterey Square. Launitz was noted for his memorial pieces found in cemeteries. He provided details of the monument in a letter to the Pulaski Monument Commission:

> Gentlemen: I herewith have the honour to submit, according to your proposals, a design for a monument to the memory of Count Pulaski,,,

It is perceived, at the first glance, that the monument is intended for a *soldier*, who is losing his life fighting. Wounded, he falls from his horse, while still grasping his sword. The date of the event is recorded above the subject. The coat of arms of Poland and Georgia, surrounded by branches of laurel, ornament the cornice of two sides, or fronts; they stand united together; while the eagle—emblem of liberty, independence, and courage—rests on both, bidding proud defiance, the eagle being the symbolic bird of both Poland and America. The allegory will need no further explanation. The cannon reversed on the corners of the die, are emblematical of military loss and mourning, while they give the monument a strong military character.

The monument is surmounted by a *Lady Liberty*, holding the banner of the "stars and stripes." The love of liberty brought Pulaski to America; for love of liberty, he fought and, for liberty, he lost his life. Thus, I thought that Liberty should crown his monument and share with him the crown of victory. The garlands surrounding the column show that Liberty now is a young and blooming maiden, surrounded with fragrant flowers.[14]

The Italian marble monument is approximately fifty-five feet tall. The monument brings Polish-Americans from across the country to Savannah to honor Pulaski, especially on the anniversary of Pulaski's death, on October 11, 1958. On this day, the first official annual pilgrimage of Polish-Americans to Savannah took place. The Pulaski Society performed honors at the monument in 1986. In 1990, some of the ornamentation from the top of the shaft fell off due to deterioration. The monument had numerous cracks and patched places. Seventy pounds of marble fell. The city, worried about stone falling on unsuspecting tourists and townspeople, set up a net around the monument to catch the marble. This started a nearly one-million-dollar and four-year restoration of the work.

It was during this restoration project that one of the more fascinating issues of Pulaski's death came to the forefront. A box with human bones was discovered at the foot of the monument. It had always been debated whether Pulaski was buried at sea or if he had been taken off the boat and buried on land. Thus, local and other historians began the big debate: where are the bones of Pulaski?

Recent examination of the papers of several officers in Pulaski's unit, the Pulaski Legion, are on microfilm as part of the collections of the letters maintained by the federal government; these have closed the debate for most. "They were asking for back pay," Polish historian Francis Kajencki, who has researched extensively Pulaski's burial, said with a laugh. "Those letters outlined their service, and I got a good bit of information from that."[15] One key element came from the papers of General Benjamin Lincoln, the American commander at the siege; a piece of correspondence in that collection was a letter from the commander of an American privateer ship, the *Wasp*. "The commander said he was anchored at Thunderbolt," said Kajencki of the letter dated October 15, 1779. "The captain said he had brought two Americans on board and one died today."[16] The letter further stated the dead soldier was then taken ashore and buried. There is consensus that Pulaski was one of those two brought onto the ship. After that, it gets a little contentious. A letter written by Captain Bullfinch states that his ship lay off Thunderbolt; he reported the burial detail of an American officer who had recently died aboard the ship and was given a funeral on land.

Kajencki steadfastly maintained Pulaski was the one taken off the ship and buried at Greenwich Plantation. "The ship's purser (supply officer) died in 1826, and his wife applied for a widow's pension," Kajencki said. "She wrote that her husband had crafted a coffin for Pulaski's body as part of his duties."[17] The decision on what to do with the body would have been pretty straightforward, according to Kajencki, a veteran who is familiar with the way the military handles bodies. "Why would they have sailed away with a body on board?" Burials at sea were not usually done with land in sight. The gravesite of Pulaski was identified by the grandson of Jane Bowen, who owned the Greenwich plantation in 1779. His bones were dug up in 1852 and moved to a vault under the Pulaski Monument.[18] These were the bones they found during the restoration of the monument. The remains were revealed to have broken bones in the right hand as well as injuries to the head and tailbone; these are similar to wounds suffered by the general. Results of DNA were inconclusive because of water damage to the remains. All of this evidence has convinced most that these were in fact the remains of Casimir Pulaski.

In 2001, the restoration of Pulaski Monument was completed. Finally, on October 9, 2005, the 226th anniversary of the Siege of Savannah, a funeral service and a final interment ceremony to honor the great Polish-American soldier were held.

Hundreds of soldiers, Revolutionary War reenactors, Polish-Americans, Polish dignitaries, and spectators marched from the remains of the Spring Hill redoubt on Martin Luther King Jr. Boulevard and Louisville Road, where now stands the Battlefield Park in memory of the Siege of Savannah, to Monterey Square. A snare drummer beat out a slow staccato as the parade began. The bells of St. John's Episcopal Church, St. John the Baptist Cathedral, and Savannah's City Hall rang out across the city. Last rites were held by a Catholic priest over the remains, and the body of Pulaski was reinterred.

"You have done a great effort to preserve the memory of this great man," said Darius Jadowski, the Polish Embassy's Minister Counselor and Ambassador Extraordinaire. "It makes us very proud to know the people in the proud state of Georgia remember the history of our great hero."[19]

The Siege of Savannah stands as a great reminder of the hope that the international community had at the time of this fledging new country: something great was possible here. The French, Haitians, Irish, Hussars, and others stood at our side to help form this more perfect union. Hopefully, we have and will continue to live up to this hope.

Colonial Road Markers: A Little Help from Our Friend

In 1735, two years after the Oglethorpe's settlement of Savannah, he began to make fortifications throughout Georgia to ensure the safety and defense of Savannah from the Spanish or French, who might use the coastal waterways to invade the British colony. In October of that year, a band of Highland Scots, recruited by Oglethorpe, sailed from Inverness, Scotland, on the ship *Prince*

A picture of the cannon that marks the beginning of the road to Darien. Tomochichi helped lay this road out.

Detail at the bottom of the Pulaski Monument.

Detail at the bottom of Pulaski Monument depicting the moment he was mortally wounded at the Battle of Savannah.

of Wales. In early January 1736, they arrived in Savannah and the Scots established a settlement they called Darien. This settlement, along with a bigger fortification on St. Simon's Island, was to protect the coast of the new colony from the Spaniards in Florida.

Also, in 1735, Oglethorpe sent troops to explore the Savannah River. He gave them an order to build at the head of the navigable part of the river. The expedition was led by Noble Jones, who created the settlement later called Augusta (Georgia's second state capital, 1785–1795, and home to the Masters Golf Tournament). With these two settlements, Oglethorpe had secured the territory north and south of Savannah to provide a first line of defense for coastal areas.

Tomochichi, the Mico of the Yamacraw tribe, who had welcomed the immigrants from England with open arms, became crucial to Oglethorpe's plan of defense. Now, with the settlements in Darien to the south and Augusta in the north, Oglethorpe needed to create roads as a means to transport reinforcements, communication, and supplies to the two new settlements. Tomochichi had fast become a friend of Oglethorpe and was influential in helping him develop a peaceful settlement amongst the Native Americans. Tomochichi also assisted Oglethorpe in laying out the road to the important Darien seaport. He used old Indian trails to show the way and make it easier for clearing the roads. This, and the road to Augusta, both of which started from this approximate spot, became the first roads in Georgia.

Each road is represented by cannons from the Savannah Armory. They were erected in 1920 by the Savannah Chapter of the Daughters of the American Revolution.

Jasper Monument: Why Do the Irish Make Such a Big Fuss About Me?

There is a saying in Savannah that everyone is Irish on St. Patrick's Day. Savannah's Irish population is a proud lot. Savannah boasts the third, second, or first largest St. Patrick's Day parade—it varies according to who you are asking and what they count. Hundreds of

View from the side of two cannons that mark the first roads in Georgia.

The Sergeant Jasper Monument in Monterey Square.

thousands of people come from all over the world to celebrate here on that day. Our fountains are turned green. A formal service of worship is held at St. John the Baptist Cathedral. A rugby tournament of teams from all over the United States is played. A Mardi Gras atmosphere hits River Street after the parade. It is the biggest event in Savannah.

As one of the preludes to the event, a ceremony is held and a wreath is laid at the Sergeant Jasper Monument in Madison Square in honor of Revolutionary War hero Sergeant William Jasper. The act that first brought him renowned attention occurred on June 28, 1776, when he rescued the flag of his regiment while defending Fort Moultrie, near Charleston. During the battle, the regiment's flag was shot from its staff and fell outside the walls of the fort. Jasper jumped the wall, braving a bombardment of the British's ships, to retrieve the banner. Amid the chaos of the battle, he calmly gathered the flag and tied it back to its staff, firmly planting it on the summit of the Fort shouting, "God save liberty and my country forever!" Jasper returned to his post and continued fighting until the British fleet retreated that night.

For this act of bravery, Governor Rutledge of South Carolina, a signer of the United States Constitution, offered Jasper a commission. Jasper, feeling he was unworthy of such an honor, due to his illiteracy, instead, accepted a sword from the Governor.

Jasper's actions at Fort Moultrie (on Sullivans Island at the entrance to the harbor of Charleston, South Carolina, originally called Fort Sullivan and constructed by Colonel William Moultrie) earned him certain privileges from his commander. With his commander's blessing, Jasper led a series of daring, small guerrilla raids on British forces in coastal Georgia. As his commander, Moultrie later recalled in his book *Memories of the American Revolution,* concerning North and South Carolina and Georgia-American Revolution, 1775–83, a struggle by which the Thirteen Colonies on the Atlantic seaboard of North America won independence from Great Britain and became the United States (also called the American War of Independence), "I had such confidence in [Jasper] that when I was in the field I gave him a roving commission and liberty to pick out his men from my brigade. He seldom would take more than six; he went out often and would return with prisoners before I knew he was gone."[20]

Soon after this event, Jasper's second heroic act occurred. At a site now known as Jasper Springs, Jasper and John Newton valiantly rescued twelve American prisoners from British soldiers. A monument to this act stands outside Savannah under a viaduct at Jasper Springs.

The third and final act for which Jasper is remembered occurred during the Siege of Savannah on October 9, 1779. On this day, the regimental flag fell and Jasper once again rushed to the rescue, but this time he was not as fortunate as at Fort Moultrie. Jasper was mortally wounded. This siege was an unsuccessful attempt to rescue Savannah from the British. On the American

Relief on the base of the monument that depicts Sergeant Jasper valiantly raising the fallen flag at Fort Moultrie.

Relief on the base of the monument that depicts Sergeant Jasper capturing the British soldiers and freeing Colonist POWs at Jasper Springs.

Relief on the base of the monument that shows the fatally wounded Jasper at the Battle of Savannah.

side, the fierce fighting claimed the lives of 200 Americans and 600 French and foreign troops. Among the dead was Count Casimir Pulaski. (Another Savannah monument honors him noted earlier.) The flag that Jasper tried valiantly to save remained in British hands as a prize of the battle. Colonel Isaac Hayne recorded the names of those who died during the assault. He listed the brave Sergeant Jasper as a casualty. The word brave was reserved for Jasper.[21]

Sixty-one years after his death, a speech romanticizing Jasper's heroism prompted the founding of the Irish Jasper Greens, a military unit formed in 1842 that fought in the Mexican War and later in the Civil War. Also, the Jasper Monument Association was formed to erect a monument to this young man. President Grover Cleveland attended the Jasper Monument unveiling ceremony in Madison Square in 1888.

The sculptor commissioned was Alexander Doyle, a well-known American artist who lived from 1857 to 1922. He has work throughout the United States and some of his best work can be found in New Orleans. He sculpted three Confederate generals: General Robert E. Lee (Lee Park 1884), General P.G. T. Beauregard (City Park 1915), and General Albert Sidney Johnston (Metairie Cemetery 1887). Doyle has another amazing work in Metairie Cemetery named *Calling the Roll*; it is of an unknown Confederate soldier.

A Doyle marble statue of Margaret Haughery, in Margaret's Park, a New Orleans woman who devoted her life to the poor, was erected in 1889, and is long thought to be the first monument to honor a female in the United States. She made her fortune in the baking business and started two orphanages. During the Civil War, Haughery became a heroine when she defied Union General Benjamin Butler by crossing Federal picket lines to deliver bread to hungry children. When she died in 1882, she left an estate of more than $30,000, all to charity. The mayor of New Orleans led the funeral procession and two Louisiana governors were pallbearers.

Doyle also sculpted the Henry W. Grady Monument in Atlanta in 1890. Grady was Atlanta's famous newspaper editor who was noted for coining the phrase "New South." Grady was the son of a wealthy merchant. When the ten-foot-tall monument was unveiled on October 21, 1891, over 25,000 people turned out for the occasion.

So, it is with great pride that the Irish hold their annual ceremony at this renowned Irish patriot's monument during the St. Patrick's Day festivities. Etched on the monument's base clearly states that Jasper was an Irish patriot. But there is one small problem: most

Plaque on the monument that calls Jasper an Irish-American soldier.

26

evidence points to the fact that Jasper was not Irish, but German. A ship's list of immigrants from the German *Palatinate* arriving in Philadelphia on October 29, 1767, contained the name "John William Jasper" and the mark of an illiterate man. There has not been any evidence found of an Irish immigrant named William Jasper. Although the Jasper Monumental Association responsible for the monument declared the statue an "Irish effort for a tribute to Irish valor…" and a huge centennial celebration of Jasper by the Irish group was held, the evidence shows that he was not Irish.

As early as 1931, suspicions that he was not Irish were written in an essay by historian Thomas Gamble.[22] In 1980, the local German Heritage Society said Jasper was of German ancestry and formally inducted him into their society. He was Johann Wilhelm Jasper, according to ship records, the Society says. A retired history professor, Fenwick Jones, who has done research on Jasper, said the man was naturalized after arriving in the American colonies. Irish, being subjects of England, did not have to be naturalized, he said.[23]

How did the Irish reply? "Sergeant Jasper came from Ireland, period," said St. Patrick's Day Parade Committee Chairman Jimmy Ray. "And I'm sticking with that—he was Irish."[24]

So the practice of laying the wreath on St. Patrick's Day continues. And really, does it matter? Because we are all Irish on that particular day.

Southern Line of Defenses Monument: No Southern Hospitality for the Brits, Y'all

The Sons of Liberty and Joseph Habersham had made the British authorities and British Governor James Wright leave and give up control of Savannah in 1776. But as General Washington's northern forces appeared to be in a stalemate with the British, the British decided on what was called a "Southern strategy." They decided that the South would have more Tories and Loyalists and would support the war effort of England. They concluded that

Picture of the marker that shows the southern boundary of British forces during the Battle of Savannah.

the South would be theirs for the taking. This would even be proven true until the southern forces were handed over to General Nathaniel Greene. The British Army invaded Savannah and reclaimed her for England on July 22, 1779.

General Benjamin Lincoln, head of the colonial army in the South, thought the loss of an important port city, such as Savannah, would not bode well for the colonists. Thus, the plans for the Battle of Savannah began to be laid. He needed a fleet to make evacuation from Savannah impossible and thereby causing the British to have no recourse but to surrender to the superior forces he was organizing. He enlisted the assistance of Charles Hector, Count D' Estaing, head of a French fleet. General Washington, seeing the importance of the battle, sent his trusted soldier Brigadier General Casimir Pulaski. The Siege of Savannah would last twenty-two days and still the British did not surrender as the colonists had hoped and requested.

At dawn on October 9, 1779, the assault of 5,500 French and American troops attacked the 2,500 fortified British forces here. Despite every effort by the American troops, the few breaches they made in the British defenses would not hold. The Count D' Estaing would be seriously injured, and Pulaski and the famed Sergeant Jasper would both be mortally wounded. Eight hundred American and French troops would die in the attack. It would be one of the bloodiest battles in the Revolutionary War. The British would hold Savannah until July 11, 1782. Only after the surrender of General Cornwallis at

Close-up of the southern boundary marker plaque.

Rotary Club Monument found on the Liberty Street divider.

Yorktown, in 1781, would the reinstated Governor Wright and the British troops evacuate Savannah.

This marker in the same square as the monument to Sergeant William Jasper serves as a reminder of the blood spilled to create a new nation, and also as a reminder that those we fight against can be every bit as brave and loyal to their cause. Sometimes, when the war is over and time passes, we find that there is much to appreciate in each other and we can become allies.

Rotary Club Monument: Four Questions for You

The world's first service club was the Rotary Club of Chicago. It was formed in 1905 by Paul P. Harris, an attorney who wanted to recreate the small town ethos of working together to promote their towns and improve their quality of life among the professionals with whom he worked. The name Rotary derived from the early practice of rotating meetings among members' offices.

The Rotary Club's popularity was to spread rapidly. Within a decade, clubs were chartered from San Francisco to New York. By 1921, Rotary Clubs had even spread internationally and could be found on six continents. Today, 1.2 million Rotarians belong to over 32,000 Rotary Clubs in more than 200 countries. The organization's distinguished reputation attracted presidents, prime ministers, and a host of other luminaries to its ranks—among them author Thomas Mann, humanitarian Albert Schweitzer, and composer Jean Sibelius.[25]

At an organizational meeting for a Savannah Rotary Club, twenty-four businessmen attended the January 5, 1914, meeting and eighteen of these men would later join. Twenty-four additional businessmen joined at the charter meeting on January 12, 1914. These forty-two men would become Charter Members of the Savannah Rotary Club.

Today, there are eleven clubs in the Savannah area. The Savannah Rotarians have contributed much to the civic life of the city. Two of their more famous members were General George C. Marshall of World War II fame and Dr. Charles H. Herty, who pioneered many new ways of making paper.[26]

Living up to their motto "Service Before Self," the Rotary has sponsored such local and varied projects as raising money for the road to Tybee Island and the local orphanage, the Bethesda Home for Boys. They promote and participate in many community service projects, such as Boy Scouts, educational fundraising, Christmas for the Poor, youth sport programs, and others have raised funds to light downtown squares, construct water fountains and landscapes in our largest park in honor of Savannah's hosting of the 1996 Sailing Olympics. The club built the fifteen-foot City Market clock. Additionally, the Georgia 6920 Rotary District, of which the Savannah Rotarians are a part, offers scholarships to international students for one year of study at Georgia colleges and universities, has operated a medical equipment transport service in order to provide medical equipment and supplies to nations all over the world, have installed wells where there was no safe drinking water, have provided training resources to teach indigenous health promoters to return to their mountain villages to instill more healthy practices,

and provided thousands of desks for schools whose students previously sat on the ground.

The monument is a Rotary wheel on a post. It was once the center piece of a fountain erected by the Rotary Club of Savannah in 1925, located at the base of the Savannah River Bridge. It stood there to welcome visitors to our city. In the 1970s, when the highway was reconfigured and the fountain removed, the Rotary wheel was relocated to its present site at Bull and Liberty Streets to commemorate the founding of the Rotary Club of Savannah on the adjacent site of the old Desoto Hotel. At the base are two plaques that have the Four-Way Test of the Rotary Clubs and members for everything they think, say, or do:

1. Is it the TRUTH?
2. Is it FAIR to all concerned?
3. Will it build GOODWILL and BETTER FRIENDSHIPS?
4. Will it be BENEFICIAL to all Concerned?

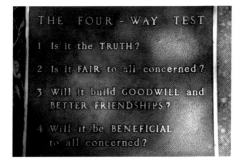

Plaque at the base of the Rotary Club Monument of the Club's Four Way Test of decision-making.

This test, adopted in the 1940s by the Rotary Clubs, if embraced by all, would and does make the world a better place.

Oglethorpe Monument:
To Dream the Impossible Dream

Savannah's official colonial story begins with the landing of the ship *Anne*. The leader of the group was General James Oglethorpe, the founder of the thirteenth colony, Georgia, and the designer of the world-renowned city plan for historic Savannah. Oglethorpe, while serving as head of a prison reform committee, had a vision. The conception of the plan in Oglethorpe's charter was for the poor in England's debtors' prisons to be brought to a new colony to have a chance to start over. The new colony was appealing to the English because it would work as a military buffer between the other colonies and the Spanish in Florida, and rid England of many of her poor, but give them a chance for a new life. Oglethorpe was a utopian visionary who saw Georgia as an opportunity to create an ideal colony.

Yet, at the time the monument committee decided to construct this sculpture in 1910, only a portrait of Oglethorpe at the state capitol was displayed in his honor. Chippewa Square, one of the more prominent places in Savannah, was chosen for his monument.

To celebrate this great man, the committee chose the renowned sculptor Daniel Chester French. He was selected over many other sculptors, including Alexander Doyle, the artist for the Jasper Statue in Monterey Square. The committee called upon accomplished

Oglethorpe standing facing the Spaniards in the south with a sword in his hand but pointed toward the ground. He is ready for diplomacy or battle, whichever his adversary chooses.

artist Gari Melchers to help choose the right sculptor. Melchers' paintings today can be found in museums across the world including major museums in Paris, Berlin, Holland, Chicago, New York, Boston, and Washington, DC, to name a few. The reason the committee approached Melchers was that he was married to Savannah artist and native Connie Lawton Mackall, and he also was working as an acquisitions advisor and purchaser for the Telfair Museum of Art. Melchers said if they were interested in a work of art that the Jasper Monument was not in the true "work of art" class. He began a subtle promotion of Daniel Chester French as the sculptor.[27]

Considering Doyle's renown and accomplishments as an artist, why did Melcher warn against him and promote French? One reason may be nothing more than the good ol' boy system. French and Melchers had both recently been elected as the first fifty members of the American Academy of Arts and Letters. They would have socialized and attended academic functions together. The deal was sealed when Melchers sent to the committee the winners of the World Exposition in Paris with French's name at the top.

French produced his first important commission for the town of Concord, Massachusetts, the famous statue *The Minute Man* of 1874. He was the leading turn-of-the-century American sculptor, with studios in Boston, Concord, Washington, DC, and New York City. His other notable public monuments include the equestrian statues of Ulysses S. Grant in Philadelphia, in 1898, and George Washington in Paris, in 1900. He also has sculptures representing Europe, Asia, Africa, and America, in front of the New York City customhouse, completed in 1907. French partnered with Henry Bacon, an accomplished monumental architect and sculpted the statue with Bacon designing the base. Three years later, Bacon and French would work together on one of their best-known works: the celebrated Lincoln Memorial in Washington, DC. Again, French sculpted the seated Lincoln and Bacon designed the building in which the sculpture was sited.

The square where Oglethorpe's statue stands was constructed in 1815. The famous bench in the movie *Forrest Gump* was located at this site. The bench was a prop and is now found in the Savannah History Museum. On the northeast side sits the Savannah Theater and across the Square is the oldest church building in Savannah, the First Baptist Church. (One wonders if the Baptists, years ago, were displeased with the sinful theater in such close proximity to their building). Historic homes, the Independent Presbyterian Church education building, a coffee house, and the Board of Education surround the rest of Chippewa Square. The Square also has a marker to early American novelist William Carruthers, but towering in the middle of it is the statue of General James Oglethorpe.

It stands at nine feet and with an eight foot tall base. Oglethorpe stands erect towering seventeen feet above viewers dressed in a general's outfit with sword turned down, ready either for battle or diplomacy. He stands ever vigilant, facing the south to protect the northern English colonies from the Spanish enemy in Florida.

The figure of Oglethorpe is bronze and rests on a stepped, inscribed, pink-gray, marble pedestal that displays garlands and pine cones. Two Italian Renaissance stone benches are on either side of the site. It was unveiled at a ceremony on November 23, 1910.

One of four lions that sits on the corners of the Oglethorpe Monument. Notice in the background the words of the Trustees Charter for the Colony of Georgia.

The charter given to Oglethorpe to start the colony is, in part, engraved on the side of the monument at a foundation. Four lions sit at each corner of the foundation; they hold before them Oglethorpe's coat of arms, the seal of the colony of Georgia, the Georgia state seal, and the seal of Savannah. Oglethorpe is proudly claimed by both Georgia and Savannah.

The Oglethorpe Monument as it stands in Chippewa Square. Notice the fine base Henry Bacon made for Daniel Chester French's sculpture of Oglethorpe.

What the monument does not say is that Oglethorpe's experiment failed. Not one person from a debtors' prison ever reached the shores of Georgia. It also does not indicate that Oglethorpe swore he would disassociate himself from the colony if slavery were legalized.[28] Additionally omitted is the fact that Oglethorpe left Georgia for England to defend himself against charges that he had mishandled the affairs of the trustees. Although exonerated of all charges, he would never return to Georgia. His attendance at trustee meetings would stop after they abandoned the principles (one of which was the prohibition of slavery) that had led to the establishment of the colony.[29] Oglethorpe was displeased that, over his objections, the trustees had lifted the ban on slavery, as he considered himself a strong advocate of its abolition. His church burial plaque would count one of his many accomplishments as "the noble example of prohibiting the importation of slaves into the Georgia colony."

The Oglethorpe Monument is dedicated to a man who is heralded in accepted history, a history told of benevolence and anti-slavery, although neither of these were actually the stories of the early Georgians. What if the colony had continued his ban on slavery? What would have happened? We will never know, but, for a brief moment, an alternative was offered.

Simple bird bath honoring Toonahowie, the adopted son of Tomochichi.

Toonahowie Birdbath: A Young Friend

Toonahowie was the nephew and adopted son of Tomochichi. Tomochichi was the Mico of the Yamacraw Indians. He had organized this tribe from various members of the Creek and Yemasee tribes to form the new tribe. Toonahowie was groomed by Tomochichi to take his place as the Mico after he died. He was taught to read and write English by Tomochichi's and Oglethorpe's translator, Mary Musgrove. Mary Musgrove's parents were English and Creek. Musgrove married into a Charleston family and lived among both the Native Americans and English. She would later become a successful businesswoman. She helped fund both Oglethorpe's military ventures against the Spanish and, later, the colonist military efforts against the British.

Toonahowie, Tomochichi, Musgrove, and Tomochichi's wife Senawki would lead the local Native Americans to accept Oglethorpe and his new colony based in Savannah. They would even travel to England with Oglethorpe (except for Musgrove, whose parents were sick) to promote positive relations with the British. On the trip they would travel with several other local Indian leaders. They made quite the impression on the British as they traveled throughout England.

Once they arrived back in Savannah after several months abroad, they met with the local Native Americans and continued to act as ambassadors for Oglethorpe and the British to their fellow Indians. Toonahowie would

The monument marks the former site of a Jewish cemetery. Notice the rocks left on top of the monument. They are a promise to remember those who were buried here.

name Cumberland Island after one of the people he'd met in England, Duke of Cumberland, William Augustus, who, as a fifteen-year-old prince, had made friends with the young Toonahowie. When Tomochichi died in 1739, Toonahowie took over the leadership. But Toonahowie would not live more than five years after Tomochichi's death. He and four other marines were attacked and captured. The Creeks caught up with Toonahowie's Yamassee kidnappers and, during the ensuing fight, Toonahowie died. He was only twenty-one.

The Yamacraws and other Native Americans welcomed the British with open arms. Yet the sad fact is the colonists would slowly break treaty after treaty with the Native Americans as they spread west, taking the land from them. After gold was found in North Georgia, the last of the Indians were relocated to the Midwest. Their land was taken. Today, we call this removal the Trail of Tears.

This birdbath monument was erected to remind us of the young Toonahowie and the families of Native Americans who welcomed the British.

Jewish Burial Ground Monument: We Remember

Oglethorpe landed in America in February 1733, and settled in Savannah only five months before two schooners, the *William* and *Sarah,* came to shore. The ships carried forty-two Sephardic Jews from Spain and Ashkenazim Jews from Germany. They were looking for safe harbor. Oglethorpe welcomed them, although the trustees were in the process of not allowing non-Christians to settle in the new colony. When challenged by the trustees about these Jewish immigrants, Oglethorpe argued that they were proving their usefulness already; in fact, a doctor among them, Samuel Nunes (also spelled Nunez) had helped greatly during an outbreak of yellow fever. The trustees followed Oglethorpe's advice and allowed the Jews to stay.[30]

But the two groups of Jews were of two very different Jewish heritages. Their liturgies were different: the Sephardic spoke Ladino, a Latin-based language, while the Ashkenazim spoke a German-based Yiddish. The differences were so great they could not come together to even build a synagogue. In 1734, an Anglican clergyman noted, "... some Jews in Savannah complained, that the Spanish Jews persecuted the German Jews in a way no Christian would persecute another Christian."[31] Eventually, the Sephardim would leave because of fears that the Spanish in Florida would invade, conquer, and then persecute them as they had experienced in Spain. This would leave only two families: the Ashkenazim Sheftall and Minis families. These are the families buried at this monument site.

Benjamin Sheftall was the patriarch of the family. His family, in July 1735, assisted in the establishment of Congregation Mickve Israel (Hope of Israel). It was the third-oldest Jewish congregation in the United States. Sheftall had been a member of the first group of Jews to arrive in Georgia. The Torah scroll they brought with them from London is still in the possession of the Savannah congregation today. In 1748,

Sheftall also had tefillin (phylacteries) brought over from England for the bar mitzvah of one of his sons, which was, according to historian Louis Schmier, "the first recorded observance of this rite in America."[32] Several members of the Sheftall family became prosperous entrepreneurs in the years preceding the American Revolution and took leading parts in the war itself. Benjamin Sheftall was one of the founders of the Union Society, the oldest charitable society in the state.

His son Mordecai would make one of the biggest contributions to the cause of the colonies during the Revolution. He was a large landowner who owned a flourishing tannery and would give one and a half acres of land for the establishment of Georgia's first large Jewish cemetery. It is referred to as the Sheftall Cemetery and, until the mid-1800s, it was open to all Jews in good standing. He also took an active part in the charitable Union Society. One of their efforts included support and guidance of the historic Bethesda Orphanage.

Sheftall, as a loyal Savannah colonist, objected to Britain's Stamp Act. Sheftall would join the Savannah Parochial Committee, a group of townspeople calling for American independence in lieu of several unfavorable British actions toward the colonies. He was elected its chairman for a term. The Parochial Committee took upon itself such functions as enforcing embargoes on molasses, corn, and slaves.[33]

When the Revolutionary War started, Mordecai Sheftall would become the highest-ranking Jewish officer, a

colonel, in the Revolutionary Army. When Georgia or the Continental Congress did not have the necessary resources, Sheftall used his own personal funds to care for the men under his command. He made loans to outfit his troops with munitions, food, uniforms, and horses. The loans would never be paid back in full and would lead to the loss of his fortune.

The Jewish Savannahians would continue their influence in Georgian and American life after the Revolutionary War. Herman Myers was a successful Jewish cigar manufacturer in Savannah. His prominence in civic and economic life is marked by his presence on the board of many Savannah banks and railroad companies. Myers served as a city alderman beginning in 1885. Breaking all stereotypes of the Deep South, Myers was mayor of Savannah from 1895 to 1907, except for a two-year period. He is said to have ushered the city of Savannah into the modern era. One contemporary account noted that, "His administration has been marked by the greatest public improvements in the history of Savannah...a magnificent new City Hall was erected which is the finest south of Richmond, Virginia."[34] The account recalled that at his funeral, in 1909, "thousands of persons from every walk in life and all ages went to the City Hall to get a last look at the man who, in life, did so much for Savannah."[35]

Another prominent Jew was the Savannah-born Rabbi Morris Samuel Lazaron, who served as a chaplain in the US Army during World War I. In 1921, he was one of four officiating chaplains attending the burial of the Unknown Soldier at Arlington National Cemetery in Washington, DC.

George Washington, responding to a letter he had received from Levi Sheftall of the Congregation Mickve Israel, made them the first Jewish community to receive a letter from a President of the United States. Washington's letter reads:

To the Hebrew Congregation of the city of Savannah, Georgia:

May the same wonder-working Deity, who long since delivering the Hebrews from their Egyptian Oppressors planted them in the promised land— whose providential agency has lately been conspicuous in establishing these United States as an independent nation—still continue to water them with the dews of heaven and to make the inhabitants of every denomination participate in the temporal and spiritual blessings of that people whose God is Jehovah.[36]

The construction of Mickve Israel Synagogue was finished on March 1, 1876. The style of Gothic Revival architecture was the work of New York architect Henry G. Harrison. It is the third oldest synagogue in the United States. Today, it is listed on the National Register of Historic Places.

The Jewish burial marker was to commemorate the 250th anniversary of Georgia in 1983. It is at the original burial plot allotted by General James Oglethorpe to the Savannah Jewish community and is made of Elberton blue granite. On the backside of the monument are the names of Jews who are known to be buried there. Such figures as Samuel Nunes' wife, the doctor who proved so valuable to Oglethorpe during the yellow fever epidemic; the mother of Mordecai Sheftall, Sheftall Sheftall, the son of Mordecai, who as a teenager assisted his father in his military duty, and others are listed. The monument states that Sheftall died young because a nurse fed him acorns and notes that another person was shot by accident.

The stones usually found on top of the memorial are placed there by Jews; according to Jewish custom, no flowers are placed at gravesites. Instead,

The back of the Jewish cemetery marker listing some of the known Jews who were once buried there. Notice Sheftall; he died from acorns his nurse had fed him.

they often place stones on the grave or tombstone. The origin of the custom is uncertain, though it may relate to ancient times when a pile of stones was used as a marker. The most common explanation is that placing stones is a symbolic act that indicates someone has come to visit and the deceased has not been forgotten.

Today, Savannah boasts three Jewish congregations, a Jewish Film Festival, a Jewish Food Festival, and a Jewish Education Alliance Center. Their Jewish ancestors who fled to America many years ago could now see that their dreams of religious freedom had become a reality in the vibrant congregations of Savannah and their presence in all aspects in the Savannah community. The Jews of today place these pebbles on the cemetery marker to let their ancestors know they are remembered.

St. Andrew's Monument: "Tyrants Fall in Every Blow"

Scotsmen landed with James Oglethorpe at the founding of Georgia in 1733. The Scots first came to the Georgia colony in large numbers because they were among the finest soldiers in the world. Oglethorpe recruited them for these military skills because he wanted to create a buffer between the Spanish in Florida and the settled colony of South Carolina. This was one of the primary rationales for giving Oglethorpe permission to establish his colony. The largest contingents of Scots first arrived, in 1735, aboard the ship *Prince of Wales* and built the seaport city now known as Darien, south of Savannah. In Darien,

Monument to the Savannah Scots.

they built Fort King George and sent a company of soldiers to man Fort Frederica on St. Simons Island. Here, the Scots played a critical role in the defeat of the Spanish in 1742, which solidified the English claim on the North American continent.

Scottish immigrants to the colonies in the eighteenth century outnumbered all others. They brought with them a strong faith. The Presbyterian Church of Savannah, today the Independent Presbyterian Church, was established in 1755 as the first Presbyterian Church in Georgia. Land for its first building was deeded by King George II of England and it was to be used by adherents of the Church of Scotland. The first building burned down in 1796, and another, modeled after St. Martin in the Fields, was built in 1800. This building burned down in 1889. Its marble baptismal font was included in the reproduction of the church in 1891.

Supervising the reconstruction of the church was prominent Boston architect William Preston Gibbons, who also worked in Savannah on several other buildings. The dedicatory sermon was appropriately entitled, "The glory of this latter house shall be greater than the former" (Haggai 2:9). William Dean Howells, writing in *Harper's Magazine* February 1919, noted, "In architecture the primacy must be yielded above every other edifice in Savannah to the famous Independent Presbyterian Church."[37]

The church had many prominent people and events occur there. The famed hymn writer Lowell Mason, writer of such hymns as "Nearer My God to Thee," "Bless be the Tie That Binds," and "When

I Survey the Wondrous Cross," among others was the organist for a time. Their first minister, John Joachim Zubly, was a member of the Continental Congress. In 1885, President Woodrow Wilson would marry the rector's granddaughter Ellen Louise Axson and they would have their ceremony in the manse of Independent Presbyterian Church.

Once a year, a Kirkin' O' the Tartans, an ancient Scottish tradition, takes place at Independent Presbyterian Church, with the Scottish clans of Savannah participating. The Beedle, or leader of the ceremony, will pull on cream-colored knee-high socks and lace, leather brogues on his feet. Around his waist he will hang a fur-covered leather pouch called a "sporran." He will head to church where he will first carry the Bible to the pulpit. Then he will carry the mace representing Christ, as he leads a processional of members to their pews. Following comes the Kirkin', the second processional after the sermon. This time the Beedle will lead a bagpiper, the chief of clans, and banner carriers to the back of the church where they will pick up their clans' tartans. Each tartan carries its own name and represents a different Scottish clan. The Beedle will command the bagpiper to play *Scotland the Brave* and usher them back down the aisle to the front of the chapel. "Gentlemen, raise your tartans," he will instruct them. They will follow orders and shout in unison, "We raise our tartans to almighty God."[38]

The monument memorializes the 250th anniversary of the city and the presence of the Scots in Savannah since 1735. The memorial displays the patron

saint of Scotland, St. Andrew, with his saltire cross. The cross would be placed on the Scottish flag. The monument also has a quote from Scotland's greatest poet, Robert Burns. It comes from the poem *March to Bannockburn*, written to commemorate the efforts of William

"TYRANTS FALL IN EVERY FOE LIBERTY'S IN EVERY BLOW."

In memory of our Scottish forbears, whose valor inspired these immortal lines by Robert Burns, this marker is gratefully dedicated by the Saint Andrew's Society of Savannah, Georgia on its 250th Anniversary.
(1737 - 1987)
3 May 1987

St. Andrews, the patron saint of Scotland, is depicted. The words in the quote are from a poem by Scottish poet Robert Burns.

Wallace and Robert Bruce in their fight for Scottish independence. This poem was made into a song and is played after every Scottish National Party convention. The Savannah Scots thought the words would resonate with their new homeland.

Tyrants fall in every foe!
Liberty is in every blow!

Today, there are many manifestations of Savannah's Scottish heritage—whether it be a Scottish pub, private school, the charitable Scottish Heritage Society of St. Andrews, the annual Scottish games (where one can watch Scottish dancing and games, such as caber toss, hammer throw or sheaf lifts), eat Scottish foods, (such as shepherd's pie or haggis), or even buy a kilt. All of it is woven into the fabric of a city and colony they came to defend many years ago.

Tomochichi Monument: Have a Little Respect

Tomochichi, the Mico of the Yamacraw tribe, has also been called the cofounder of Georgia. He was a tall man with a demeanor that befitted the leader of his tribe. We do not know what his first thoughts were when he saw the ship *Anne* making its way up the Savannah River. What we do know is that he chose to embrace these strangers from another land and form an alliance with them. He would become a guide, personal friend, and supporter of General James Oglethorpe. He helped to make the settling of Georgia easier for these immigrants and kept the threat of warring Native Americans away.

One of his contributions to the settlers is found in Madison Square. Two cannons mark Ogeechee Road, the first road laid out in Georgia. The plaque says the road was laid out with the assistance of Tomochichi. Upon Tomochichi's death, in 1739, Oglethorpe decided to build a monument sensitive to the Native American culture. Tomochichi was buried in the middle of Wright Square, with a stone pyre creating a monumental mound over his grave. This grave could be said to be the first monument in Georgia.

Gordon Monument: Choo Choo

Another leader of the community, born fifty-five years after Tomochichi's death, was William Washington Gordon. His father, Ambrose Gordon, served in the cavalry in the Revolutionary War. Gordon was the first graduate of West Point from Georgia. He won election to the Georgia Legislature, first as a representative in 1835 and then as a senator in 1838. In addition, from 1834 to 1836, he served as the mayor of Savannah. His son, William Washington Gordon II, called "Willie," served during the Civil War and as a brigadier general during the Spanish-American War. He and Eleanor "Nellie" Kinzie of Chicago, Illinois, were married in 1857 and became the parents of Juliette Gordon Low, the founder of the Girl Scouts. The Gordon family for four generations were proud European Americans.

William Washington Gordon's greatest achievement was as president of the Central of Georgia Railroad and

Banking Company. The construction of a railroad from Savannah to the interior became crucial to the economy of Georgia in 1833. The dreaded Charlestonians had completed a 136-mile rail line from the port of Charleston to Hamburg, a town directly across the Savannah River in Augusta. This new railroad, the longest in the world at that time, threatened to divert the upland cotton export trade to Charleston. The cotton previously had been transported down the Savannah River from Augusta to Savannah. This would have destroyed or severely damaged the Savannah economy.

Gordon knew it was more important to Savannah to build a railroad than for him to be the mayor, so he resigned and became president of the Central of Georgia Railroad. Gordon worked hard to bring about the completion of a rail line that would reach into Georgia's central cotton belt in late 1836. Even when the financial panic of 1837 threatened the completion of the rail line, they steadily moved forward and, by May 1839, seventy-six miles of track had been laid. Gordon supervised construction, negotiated rights-of-way with planters, and dealt with labor disputes. Worn down by his labors, Gordon died in March 1842 at the age of forty-six.[39] He did not live to see the last spike driven, in 1843, but his labors had saved the Savannah economy.

The proud railroad men had lost their faithful leader. They were determined to show their appreciation for Gordon, as well as their own ascendency in the world. In 1883, a magnificent cenotaph, constructed in

The William Washington Gordon Monument in Wright Square. He was a state senator, mayor of Savannah, and first president of the Central of Georgia Railroad.

Savannah's Wright Square by the Central of Georgia Railway, was dedicated as a memorial to first company president and longtime leader Gordon. One side of the monument bears this description:

> The pioneer of works of internal improvement in his native State and first President of the Central of Georgia Railroad and Banking Company of Georgia, to which he gave his time, his talents, and finally his life.

The site was probably chosen because of its prominence—the County Courthouse is adjacent to the Square.

One of the leading architects of his day, William Van Brunt was chosen to design the monument. In 1899, he became president of the American Institute of Architects for a one-year term. A resident of Boston, he was the architect of Harvard's Memorial and Weld Halls, as well as St. John's Memorial Chapel at the Episcopal Divinity School, Cambridge, Massachusetts, and Cambridge Public Library, also in Cambridge. He would work on at least two monuments with celebrated sculptor John Quincy Adams Ward: the Ether Monument (marking the discovery of ether) of 1867, in the Boston Public Garden, and the Yorktown Memorial, Yorktown, Virginia, of 1881.

Later, Van Brunt would move to Kansas City from Boston to design commissions for the grand stations that Union Pacific Railroad needed in western cities like Ogden, Utah, which was completed in 1889, but burned

Detail of the top of the monument.

A train depicted on the side of the Gordon Monument.

down in 1923; Denver, Colorado, of 1895 and rebuilt in 1912, and Omaha, Nebraska, in 1899, but replaced in 1931. He obviously had developed rapport and connections in dealing with railroad men when he took the Gordon Monument project.

The monument, which had many of the symbols of the Greene and early Confederate memorials that were alarming to the taste of Savannahians and not much of the realism of the other accepted statues of Savannah, was gladly received by the railroad men. They were men of the here and now with a vision of the future and probably did not hold to the more refined, conservative taste—at least when it came to a more modern monument style. They also led the city to have what can only be called "convenient amnesia."

The monument was built in the center of the Square on top of Tomochichi's grave/memorial. Despite pictures of the Tomochichi grave in the center of the Square and a popular map showing it there, the *Savannah Morning News* wrote his grave could be found in the corner of the square. The article also asks about the rock mound in its center. That was a long-past remnant of a community project to enliven the squares and rock mounds that at one time were found in several squares. But no evidence of this community project can be found. All evidence, most of which could be found at that time, point to the grave being in the center of the square, but this appeared to be temporarily forgotten.[40] The memorial to Savannah's greatest railroad man was literally built on the memory and body of Savannah's most prominent Native American.

A few years after the memorial to Gordon was built, the murmurings started. What had they done to Tomochichi!? The Gordon family distanced themselves from the erection place of the Wright Monument. When General W.W. Gordon Jr. was asked about his father's monument, he said the family, who were not consulted, would have preferred the monument to be in the empty Chippewa Square. A quote from an interview says, "By rights, Tomochichi should occupy the site on which now stands the monument to my father. I have no doubt this is the exact location of the old mico's grave."[41] General Gordon's wife Nellie was president of the Georgia Society of Colonial Dames; under her leadership, they began to raise money for a new monument to Tomochichi.

Sixteen years after the Gordon Monument was completed, the Colonial Dames held their annual meeting at the home of famed Juliette Gordon Low, founder of the Girl Scouts and granddaughter of W.W. Gordon. The Dames marched from that home on Lafayette Square to Wright Square to unveil the new monument to Tomochichi. The memorial to Tomochichi consists of a granite fragment displaying an inscribed bronze plaque. The inscription reads:

> In memory of Tom-o-chi-chi.
> The mico of the Yamacraws, The
> Companion of Oglethorpe, and
> the Friend and Ally of the Colony
> of Georgia.

A simple monument in keeping with Native American tradition, it is said the granite was chosen to symbolize the Mico's strong and rugged character. It is possible this is the only memorial erected for a Native American by descendants of European settlers.[42] W.W.

THE BULL STREET MONUMENTS

A simple granite monument that sits in the corner of Wright Square in honor of Tomochichi.

Gordon had many accomplishments in his life but maybe the greatest thing he ever did was to raise a family who were concerned with doing their best to right a wrong.

Bull Sundial:
Building a Better Tomorrow

After General James Edward Oglethorpe first landed on the coast of Georgia, he soon went to Charleston to meet with the royal governor and others to gather information and assistance regarding where he might go to create the first settlement in Georgia. It was in Charleston that Oglethorpe would encounter and ask for assistance from Colonel William Bull. The Colonel would later become governor of South Carolina, but for now was a rising star in the Charleston community.

Plaque on the Tomochichi Monument; notice the arrowheads and peace pipe details.

A sundial to commemorate Colonel William Bull, who as an engineer took Oglethorpe's plan for the city of Savannah and made it real. Bull Street, where the sundial sits, was named after Colonel Bull.

One of four mosaics surrounding the Bull Sundial. This one depicts a map of Savannah in 1754.

Colonel Bull knew the coastal land of Georgia well and helped steer Oglethorpe and his expeditionary group in exploring the coast for a proper place to bring the new colonists. Governor Johnson had suggested a place further south than Savannah, but Oglethorpe decided it was too close to the Spanish in Florida for such a young settlement. He decided on Yamacraw Bluff instead (where Savannah now stands). Colonel Bull, because of his training in engineering, was the early colony's architect and engineer. He oversaw the construction of the first homes and buildings.

By far, Bull's greatest contributions were his counsel and the actual laying out of the city plan that Oglethorpe envisioned. This urban layout is internationally known as the Oglethorpe Plan, and one of Savannah's main streets is named after Colonel Bull. The Bull Monument consists of a sundial and a mosaic map of Savannah in 1734, by Peter Gordon, who also had traveled with Oglethorpe and Bull on the first expeditionary trip. It is hard to imagine this many years later of a young engineer with a plan of grids and squares in hand, looking at a forest and saying, "Yes, we will build a city." He probably could not conceive that the plan would one day be touted worldwide—or maybe he did...

Greene Monument:
One Yankee We Like

Johnson Square is the first square laid out by General James Oglethorpe. You will find in the square several plaques from engineers, city planners, and

Greene Monument stands in Savannah's first square. The obelisk challenged the aesthetic sensibilities of some Savannahians.

landscape societies honoring the design of downtown. The grid of squares created by Oglethorpe is studied and appreciated worldwide. In this Square you will also find, under the massive oaks, two fountains on the east and west sides. On the south side, you will find a sundial in honor of Colonel William Bull, whose name is on Savannah's most prominent street. In the middle of the square is a monument to General Nathanael Greene. Greene was one of George Washington's most capable generals.

Greene was a "fighting" Quaker who went against the pacifist teachings of his faith to join in the battle for American independence. This zeal for the military life would lead to his expulsion from the Quakers in 1773. When the war began,

Greene was a private in the militia. In August 1774, Greene helped organize a local militia known as the Kentish Guards. His participation in the group was challenged because he had a slight limp and it was thought he did not look like a professional soldier. He eventually won over his troops, began to study military tactics, and to teach himself the art of war. He worked as quartermaster for Washington's army, an under-appreciated job considering the fledgling nation had little money and no real structure to raise money for an army. Nevertheless, he handled his job well.[43]

The war was not going well in the south for the colonists. A leadership change was needed. Washington listed

Greene as his choice as the head of the Southern Army. The Continental Congress chose Washington's rival, Horatio Gates. General Gates, who had a questionable but flamboyant career, would lose a major battle in which he fled, leaving his army to itself. The next time, Congress decided to entrust the choice of leadership to Washington. On October 5, 1780, it resolved "that the Commander-in-Chief be and is hereby directed to appoint an officer to command the southern army, in the room of Major General Gates."[44] Washington did not delay in making his selection and chose Greene to be the leader. The Congress approved the appointment, giving Greene command over all troops from Delaware to Georgia. He was now Washington's general of the Southern Army and second in command.

Greene chose to fight what he called a "fugitive war," a term he invented. His troops would be in constant movement, avoiding the enemy, not attacking them. This would give no clear target to the opposing army. It also gave the enemy no decisive battles to win and report back to England. The few skirmishes they did have were at places and times that Greene chose. The strategy worked and made British General Cornwallis leave the Carolinas in disgust in favor of the more comfortable confines of Virginia.[45]

After independence was gained, Greene twice refused the post of Secretary of War. He was offered property by several Southern colonies for his wartime services. In 1785, Green decided to settle on an estate, Mulberry Grove, fourteen miles north of Savannah. He died there of sunstroke at forty-three years of age on June 19, 1786. His wife Catherine (Caty) continued to operate the estate after his death. She was also considered one of Savannah's leading socialites. At the Mulberry Grove estate, she entertained such friends as Washington and the Marquis de Lafayette. But probably her most significant guest for Savannah and the South's history was Eli Whitney. Whitney, while staying at Mulberry Grove, modified the cotton gin to make the

Another view of the Greene Monument.

processing of cotton easier and, therefore, more lucrative, opening the door to what would become the Cotton Empire.

The monument was at first for Greene, as well as another Revolutionary War hero, Casimir Pulaski. The monument committee had hoped to build monuments for each man, but the money was not there, so they made the memorial to represent them both. The monument was to be unveiled as part of the nationwide fifty-year anniversary celebration of the Revolutionary War. The founding fathers and mothers were slowly dying off and there was a perceived need to keep the revolutionary fire alive. The Marquis de Lafayette was traveling throughout the new nation to promote this renewal of patriotic fervor for the country. Everywhere he went celebrations were held and many monuments to honor heroes of the Revolution were erected. In 1825, he came to Savannah with much fanfare and laid the cornerstone for the Greene\ Pulaski Monument. This was to be the first civic monument of Savannah.

The designer of the monument was architect William Strickland, considered by many to be America's first great native-born architect. His work, in 1818, for the Second Bank of the United States with a design based on the Parthenon in Athens is found in many American art history books. The Second Bank was a seminal work in the history of neoclassicism in the United States. With this important commission, Strickland was established in Philadelphia as a professional architect. During a career spanning over forty-five years, William

Strickland proved himself to be versatile and talented as an architect, engineer, and surveyor.

He worked in nine different architectural styles. Strickland was one of the first to promote steam locomotives on railways. In his youth, he proved his mastery as a landscape painter, illustrator for periodicals, theatrical scene painter, engraver, and pioneer in aquatint. He later moved to Nashville, Tennessee, where his Egyptian-influenced design of the First Presbyterian Church, now the Downtown Presbyterian Church, was controversial. Today, it is widely recognized as a masterpiece and an important evocation of the Egyptian Revival style. Strickland is buried within the walls of his final and self-proclaimed best, and arguably greatest, work, the Tennessee State Capitol.

Strickland's interest in the Egyptians can be seen in his design for the Greene Monument. The design was in the Egyptian needle format: an obelisk of white New York marble, fifty feet tall. Despite Strickland's repeated successes, this monument to Greene and Pulaski was not understood in Savannah. There was not an appreciation of Egyptian Revival. What Savannahians saw was a plain piece of marble pointed upward. There were only a few obelisks found in funeral and civic monuments in the United States at this time. The most famous obelisk in Washington, DC, honoring President George Washington was not erected until 1884. This was a "cutting-edge" monument. Savannahians' aesthetics were offended by such a plain and odd-shaped monument. The complaints were frequent and ongoing.

Apparently, the completion of the Washington Monument, on December 6, 1884, did not assuage these feelings. This is why in 1886, with the erection of the Pulaski monument and in response to chronic complaints, bronze plaques were added and unveiled at a large ceremony, with Jefferson Davis as the guest of honor. This would not be the end of the saga for this monument, however. In 1901, the Society of the Cincinnati of Rhode Island, Greene's birthplace, worried that his burial place was unknown and felt that they should see to it that their distinguished member was properly buried with a monument to demonstrate his importance to American history. When they came to Savannah to do this, local historians and

The Mercer Bench in Johnson Square.

Bronze relief of Greene added later.

records did not indicate where in fact Greene had been buried. After much searching they found, in one of the brick vaults in Colonial Cemetery, a coffin plate with his name on it. They assumed, but could not prove, that the remains were those of Greene. The Rhode Islanders had, at first, thought that his remains would be returned to his home state, but a survey of his descendants determined they would like him to stay in Savannah.[46] The general and his son were reburied under the monument in honor of Greene in Johnson Square.

The first monument for Savannah would presage many of the other monuments' issues and development: a design that people did not like, hard to raise enough money, a noted architect, burial questions, changes added to the original design, and other issues would be revisited with various monuments. But through all the various problems, a civic pride is found in the telling of their history. Savannah was set to begin the creation of monuments communicating their story to the visiting world.

Mercer Bench: Sit and Listen Awhile

Savannah has foodie, architectural, African-American heritage, movies of Savannah, dolphin, riverboat, historic homes, garden, and every other imaginable type of tours. There is sure to be a Johnny Mercer tour at any moment. We have two monuments, one grave, and one marker already commemorating one of Savannah's favorite sons. His grave is in historic

Bonaventure Cemetery, which was voted one of the most beautiful cemeteries in the world. A historical marker stands by his childhood home at 226 East Gwinnett Street. A statue, talked about elsewhere, is in Ellis Square by City Market. Here in Savannah's first square sits a bench dedicated to the man and his music.

The bench was donated by the national Johnny Mercer Foundation. The mission of the Johnny Mercer Foundation (JMF) is to support the discipline of songwriting in the tradition of the Great American Songbook as exemplified by the life and work of Johnny Mercer: lyricist, composer, performer, collaborator, and producer. The Foundation continues Mercer's legacy by partnering with individuals and organizations dedicated to celebrating and nourishing the disciplines he mastered, and the causes he and Ginger Mercer championed.[47]

The bench was donated in 2002. It is crescent shaped with a copy of a self-drawn silhouette of Mercer made of Carrera marble, of which Mercer was fond. It has inscribed various information about him and lists some of his more popular songs. "I'm thrilled to death by it," said Nancy Mercer Gerard, daughter of Juliana Mercer, Johnny's sister. "Johnny attended Christ Church Episcopal. His father was an officer at Savannah Bank, and Mercer Realty and Insurance is right around the corner...," she added. "Johnny would have walked through that part of Johnson Square literally thousands of times."[48]

Although Mercer does not walk around these parts anymore, his music and his spirit can be heard in the whispers of the wind blowing through the swaying gray moss hanging from the large oak trees found in the square.

The top of the Mercer Bench. A doodle of Mercer drawn by Mercer.

II
THE
RIVER STREET
MONUMENTS

River Street is where Georgia's European history begins. It is the key to the history of Savannah. Oglethorpe landed here, slaves were brought here. Today, Savannah is the fourth largest port in the United States. The warehouses that line River Street, once filled with imports and exports, are now a tourist destination with boutiques, bars, and restaurants. The history of Savannah trying to exert its economic prowess is found on Factors Walk: the Cotton Exchange (which once set the price of cotton), a monument recognizing part of Savannah's influential maritime history; down the river is the "new" port and across the river is the International Trade and Convention Center. Also, the river is where Savannah has and does welcome the world. Here you find the Olympic Torch and *Waving Girl*. There is also the World War II monument representing Savannah's contributions to this global struggle against evil.

African-American Monument with City Hall hovering above.

WE WERE STOLEN SOLD AND BOUGHT TOGETHER FROM THE AFRICAN CONTINENT WE GOT ON THE SLAVE SHIPS TOGETHER. WE LAY BACK TO BELLY IN THE HOLDS OF THE SLAVE SHIPS IN EACH OTHERS EXCREMENT AND URINE TOGETHER. SOMETIMES DIED TOGETHER. AND OUR LIFELESS BODIES THROWN OVERBOARD TOGETHER TODAY WE ARE STANDING UP TOGETHER WITH FAITH AND EVEN SOME JOY

MAYA ANGELOU

Poet Maya Angelou's amended words describing the Middle Passage.

The African-American Monument on River Street. Notice the chains at the feet. The monument sits at the place where slaves first set foot in America.

African-American Monument: "We Have Come Over a Way that with Tears Has Been Watered"

The Actual Story

The story goes that Dr. Abigail Jordan was sitting on a bench in Morrell Park on River Street taking in the sights when a conversation that would change the next eleven years of her life took place. She was a retired Savannah State University professor and had recently founded a group called the Consortium of Doctors. As she was sitting on the bench, she was looking at the famous *Waving Girl* statue and noticing that the girl's trusted dog had a place in the pantheon of Savannah monuments. Two young African-American women approached her and wondered aloud why the city of monuments did not seem to have a monument that represented black people. Dr. Jordan realized, as she started to reply to their query, that there was not one monument of an African-American or that honored the black community's contributions to Savannah. She was shocked and embarrassed. But she was also deeply moved: she would not be responsible, by passivity, to continue to allow the community to have no monument. Thus began her eleven-year journey.

In 1991, it struck Dr. Abigail Jordan that out of Savannah's approximately forty-three monuments, not one acknowledged the contributions of African-Americans to the city. The closest thing to such an acknowledgment was the cobblestone street on which she and others were walking. "History has it that these stones were laid by the hands of slaves who selected and adjusted the odd-shaped rocks that would accommodate the pounding of human and animal feet," she later stated. "In many instances, blood and flesh from the hands and fingers of the slaves were left in the mortar that still holds the stony material together today."[49] Her meditations upon this revelation, and an inability to point out for visitors to Savannah a monument denoting the African-American presence, created in Jordan a determination that became the central driving force of her life. In the same year that she began her crusade to place on River Street a monument dedicated to Savannah's African-American legacy, Jordan was also one of the founders of the Consortium of Doctors, a group of black women doctorates dedicated to helping remove barriers to education and employment among other black women.[50] At its first induction ceremony on Saturday, July 27, 1991, the Consortium welcomed approximately fifty-four members. Eleven years after, in 2002, she would celebrate this monument on the same day Saturday, July 27, when Jordan's dream to see the monument unveiled on River Street first became a reality. Media representatives from around the world either attended the event in person or scheduled phone interviews with Jordan to report the historic event. Clearly, Dr. Jordan's decade-long battle, begun in one century and concluded in the next, is a harbinger of a better world for all.

Surprisingly, one of her chief nemeses during her quest was Floyd Adams Jr., the first African-American mayor in Savannah. It is not known exactly why he was such a thorn in the flesh for Dr. Jordan, but one can venture a few guesses. Dr. Jordan could at times be caustic. Mayor Adams and she appeared to have a personality conflict. Secondly, Dr. Jordan originally wanted to include significant black Savannahians as civil rights heroes listed on a wall surrounding the monument, The Scroll of Perseverance. Mayor Adams and many of his friends were not included in the list. Thirdly, Dr. Jordan was not someone whom Adams could control and this project was to be one of the most significant undertakings to promote the heritage of black Savannahians. Whatever the reasons, he consistently threw roadblocks in Dr. Jordan's path. Some were slights: at a city meeting, Dr. Jordan approached the podium to speak about the monument, but Mayor Adams told her she could not come to the podium until called. After Dr. Jordan sat back down, Mayor Adams called for an adjournment of the meeting. He raised objections over sculptor Dorothy Spradley, the artist chosen to create the monument, stating she was not black and maybe this monument should have a black artist. One of the most bizarre incidences was when Mayor Adams went to a meeting of the African-American Monument Association, a grassroots citizens group who raised funds for the monument. Once Mayor Adams arrived, he explained to the association he was replacing Dr. Jordan as their president (an authority he did not have). Another unintentional roadblock was the forming of a new committee to review and approve all monuments and their designs and sites. The committee made rules that no living person's name could be on a monument. This stipulation meant the loss of the heroes' wall. Dr. Jordan met with this committee several times to discuss the location of the monument. Ironically, Dr. Jordan was asking approval for the first monument to honor African-Americans from a committee that was all white at the time.[51] The committee eventually approved Spradley's design.

But the final and most significant conflict was over the words of Maya Angelou that were to be etched on the side of the monument. The monument depicts waves of an ocean superimposed with outstretched, shackled hands in agony or prayer on the base of it.

This represents the Middle Passage: the name for the voyages of slaves kept in the bottom of ships on their ways to America. Many slaves died of malnutrition, disease, and suicide on this voyage. Thus, Maya Angelou's words were chosen to be inscribed on the monument,

> We were stolen, sold and bought
> together from the African
> continent. We got on the slave

ships together. We lay back to belly in the holds of the slave ships in each other's excrement and urine together, sometimes died together, and our lifeless bodies thrown overboard together.

The mayor and others were concerned about such explicit language on a monument. Would it be offensive to tourists? Shouldn't the words be uplifting? Yes, it may be history, but it is not history that needs to be front and center. It was a debate of what some call "touristory," the history we choose to tell visitors to our city, our story. If we tell stories that may put us in a negative light, will tourists and entrepreneurs want to invest and come back? The debate raged back and forth threatening to derail the monument. The story even appeared in national and international newspapers. Finally, the President of the Consortium of Doctors called Maya Angelou and asked if she would change the words to be more acceptable. She graciously agreed and added these words "That was

yesteryear. Today, we are a family united, free, moving forward in expectation of a brighter tomorrow." At the City Council's final vote on the monument, African-American Alderman David Jones stated, "Mr. Mayor this is it—the monument is approved. This is it; are we clear with that?" Mayor Adams replied, "This is it." Mayor Adams would not attend the unveiling ceremony.[52]

On Saturday, July 7, 2002, more than 300 people packed onto Rousakis Plaza behind City Hall to dedicate the monument Dr. Jordan had envisioned. It was to be the city's first to honor African-Americans. There were songs, poems, drums, and speeches. Jordan listened to it all, but didn't address the crowd. "I've said enough," she told a reporter afterward. "After eleven years of talking, don't you think I've said enough?"[53] One lone protestor held a fluorescent sign: "Wipe the 'excrement' off of Savannah's monuments" was written on one side. The other side read: "We refuse to sit upon your stool of everlasting repentance."

Today, the monument stands on the spot where slaves were first "welcomed" to and first placed their feet in America. The statue of an African-American family huddled together, looking back to Africa from where they came, with the chains of slavery at their feet, stands as a witness to humanity's power to perform horrible deeds, but also the power of the human spirit to overcome the greatest obstacles. The monument is a testament to the courage of Savannah's black community and their work to make our community whole. It is also the manifestation of what one stubborn individual can do. And if Dr. Jordan was ever on River Street again and asked about a monument to the Savannah black community, she could say with a wry smile on her face that it is just down the road a bit.

World War II Monument: A World Apart

When Japan bombed Pearl Harbor on December 7, 1941, the next day's front page broke the news to readers. And the war truly hit home two days later in Savannah when a four-deck headline informed readers that a local boy had been killed in the bombing: Sergeant G. K. Gannam killed in Hawaii. He became Savannah's first fatality of the war.

The contributions of Savannah to the World War II effort were three-fold. The creation of the Mighty Eighth Air Force here at the local American Legion lodge, the building of Liberty ships, and the 400 men who gave their lives in the war. It was known that an air force like one never seen before would be needed

Shackled, outstretched hands on the base of the African-American Monument. Notice the waves behind the hands, symbolizing the Middle Passage.

Shackled prayer hands on the base of the African-American Monument.

World War II Monument. "A World Apart" is the theme.

to take the air war to Germany. Luftwaffe was battle experienced and, but for a brief setback in the Battle of Britain, it was dominant. It was also known that the base available for an aerial onslaught on Germany would have to be stationed in England, our ally. A small group of men meeting at Savannah's American Legion Hall began the activation of a new force on January 2, 1942. The new force was located at Hunter Army Air Field; Colonel Asa N. Duncan was the first commander. The Mighty Eighth would eventually number 350,000 men and women with over 54,000 either killed in combat or taken prisoner.

The Mighty Eighth was comprised of forty-eight bomber groups, twenty-one fighter groups, and three photo reconnaissance groups. Each of these groups, in turn, were composed of a number of squadrons.

Later in 1942, the Eighth's headquarters, as part of the US Army Air Forces (USAAF), moved to England, where its base of operations remained until the war's end in 1945. The mission of the Eighth was the heavy bombardment of strategic and military targets in Nazi-occupied Europe and Germany. The valor of the Eighth Air Force flight crews, who suffered the highest casualty rate of all American forces (12 percent), is well documented. The Mighty Eighth's heavy bombers and fighters played a key role in disrupting Germany's war effort and contributed substantially to the Allied victory. One of the reasons for their heavy casualty rates was that when they started the bombings in Europe, the fighter planes who escorted the bomber planes did not have big fuel tanks and therefore could only travel part of the mission with the bombers. Despite this, the Mighty Eighth is distinguished by the fact that they were never turned back from a mission or battle. One of the bomber pilots was actor Jimmy Stewart, who had just appeared in the movie *Mr. Smith Goes to Washington* when he'd joined the service even before Pearl Harbor. He rose to command his own squadron as a bomber pilot and flew twenty combat missions, including one to Berlin. Another fighter was Chuck Yeager, the first pilot to travel faster than the speed of sound in 1947.

Probably the most renowned of their commanders was General James H. Doolittle, a Medal of Honor recipient, who assumed command of the 8th Air Force on January 6, 1944.

The Eighth Air Force on September 18, 1947, was reorganized into a new fighting force called the Army Air Force. The Eighth Air Force continues to be an effective strategic tool. It is not gone. An estimated 650,000 have served in it since World War II. Today, Savannah celebrates this force with a large and remarkable museum in the suburban town of Pooler.

The second Savannah contribution was the Liberty Ships. Before the United States declared war, President Franklin Roosevelt wanted to assist England and his good friend Winston Churchill. The US public and Congress were in an isolationist mood and wanted to let Europe's problem stay Europe's problems. President Roosevelt decided, at the risk of our declared neutrality, to send supplies in lieu of troops. So, unofficially, he enlisted seven port cities to build supply ships to aid the Allied effort. One of those cities was Savannah. Security became so important that the mayor and councilmen declared the entire port within the city off limits to the general public. Seventy different types of ships were attacked by German U-boats off the East Coast in an attempt to hamper supply lines to Europe and to intimidate the Americans.

Thus, before war was even declared, Savannah had been involved in supplying the Allies. Workers at the Southeastern Shipyard in Savannah constructed eighty-eight Liberty Ships. These legendary workhorse ships carried troops, arms, and supplies to US and Allied forces in all theaters of the war. Many of the ships constructed in Savannah were named after Georgia cities and prominent figures in Georgia history. Ships named *Florence Martus* and *James Oglethorpe* supplied 1.25 million tons of vital supplies, including bombs, munitions, tanks, assault boats, medical supplies, food, lumber, steel, and fabricated bridges to our Allies in Europe.[54] The five holds of a Liberty Ship could carry the contents of 300 railroad cars, 2,840 jeeps, or 440 Sherman tanks. The first vessel launched was the *James Oglethorpe* on November 20, 1942. On March 11, 1943, the vessel sailed from New York City with the forty-ship convoy designated Halifax 229. Five days later, a pack of eight German U-boats attacked the convoy. The heavily loaded *Oglethorpe* was severely damaged by a torpedo fired by U-91 and it sank the following day. As the European theater of war ended, the Savannah shipyards built eighteen smaller ships, known as the AV-1, which were utilized in the Pacific campaign.[55]

The third contribution Savannah made to the war effort was the blood of her youth. Starting with Pearl Harbor and going on to the final days of the war in the Pacific, 400 men from Chatham would lose their lives in the "Good War." Many more would fight and see the horrors of war and face spiritual and physical wounds that they carried forward into the rest of their lives. They traveled to lands to fight and die in places that they

View from the River Street side.

had only read or heard about in books to defend their country. Savannah civilians and soldiers alike came together with the rest of the nation to end a modern tyranny of hate and violence.

Since Savannah had been so involved with World War II, you would expect this city of monuments would have built one soon after the war. The fact is that a monument did not come into existence until 2011. The design for the monument was created by Eric Meyerhoff, one of Savannah's leading architects. Meyerhoff has left his architectural mark on Savannah. Savannah has also left its mark on his architectural eye. He said of Savannah, "As one walks from square to square, passing each building, discovering a different nuance of detailing, from the eaves to the railings and stairs, the visual-architectural experience can be as overwhelming to the eye as a symphony is to the ear."[56] He designed Rousakis Plaza on River Street and he

World War II Monument. The monument has a map of the world inlaid in gold. Europe and Asia are pictured here.

helped restore a number of historic buildings: the old Central of Georgia station, Massie School, the Oliver Sturges House on Reynolds Square and the First African Baptist Church. His firm designed the Fine Arts Building at Armstrong Atlantic State University and the Marine Science Education Center at Skidaway Island.[57]

In 2003, then City Manager Michael Brown asked Meyerhoff to help local veterans build a World War II monument that would be placed near Hunter Army Airfield. The project was never completed, but as Meyerhoff said, "it did create a concept."[58] In 2010, now seventy-nine years old and retired for several years, Meyerhoff once again found himself with the opportunity to design the monument.[59] His concept was "Worlds Apart." A globe divided into two represents the two theaters of war as well as a world torn asunder by this seemingly all inclusive war. The names of Chatham County residents who died in the war were to be listed on the inside of the two walls of the divided globe. The original site was to be Oglethorpe Square, but it was moved to River Street after some debate about its compatibility with the neighboring historic homes. River Street, in the end, seemed the most appropriate location, since it was where the Liberty Ships were built and an area that tourists frequented. The guiding force behind the monument has been the Chatham County Veterans Council, who raised over a million-dollars, showing once again the resourcefulness of our soldiers.

The actual construction was left to noted designer and sculptor Kim Brandell. "I've made many globes before, this is the first one that is a memorial."[60] His previous globes can be seen in front of the Trump Towers in New York City and the entrance of the Port of Miami headquarters in Florida. A well-established sculptor, his most notorious project may be the "village under the sea" called *Neptune Memorial Reef.* The work has been featured on the *Today Show* and other programs.

In the end, the City of Monuments finally has honored its contributions to World War II. It is a proud, modern monument standing twenty feet tall, made of steel and copper. It sits on the waterfront to honor the veterans and the future they preserved. It also sits for us to contemplate a war that tore the world apart and of those who lost their lives a long way from home.

Steamship Savannah Monument: We Are Not Just Blowing Smoke Here

Savannah's port is one of the biggest and most important. The bluff overlooking the Savannah River is where the colony began and where a significant amount of its economy has always come. Today, River Street is a world-renowned tourist destination. One could sit in a restaurant eating or stand on a balcony of a hotel overlooking the Savannah River watching cargo ships from all over the world pass. So it is no surprise to find, in American nautical history, ships that have borne the name *Savannah.*

The Propeller Club is an organization whose membership comprises a cross section of the maritime and associated industries throughout the United States and in many cities overseas. "Propeller" in the name refers to the propulsion of ships, and is symbolic of the driving force of the nation's heavily maritime-reliant economy. The Propeller Club was organized in 1923, in New York City. In 1927, the club went national, calling itself the Propeller Club of the United States, with individual member clubs designated as "Ports." The Port of Savannah, Port No. 23, was organized in February 1933. The Propeller Club has been responsible for two monuments on River Street: an anchor fountain to the seamen who have lost their lives at sea and the Ships of Savannah Monument.

The Ships of Savannah Monument or the name I fondly use, "ship on a stick," is dedicated to four of the most prominent ships to use the Savannah name. The monument is a fountain with bronze historical markers on a two-foot-high wall surrounding it. In the center is a tin model of arguably the most famous ship of Savannah, the SS *Steamship Savannah*. The reason I call it "ship on a stick" is the model stands on a tin pole in the center of the fountain. The SS *Steamship Savannah* represents the entrepreneurial spirit of the city. Whether it be in the building of canals, railroads, planes, or the invention of the cotton gin, paper, backhoes, or the aesthetic creations of the Savannah College of Art and Design, or Paula Deen, Savannah has always been open to the spirit of enterprise and innovation. The SS *Steamship Savannah*

was no exception. But, some thought it might be a bridge too far or more precisely a steam coffin.[61]

Moses Rogers was the captain who proposed to take the first steamship across the Atlantic Ocean. This had never been done before, partly because people were afraid that wooden ships and fire from the steam engine did not mix. But Rogers believed it could be done and the *Steamship Savannah* should be the first. Rogers sought backing from the wealthy shipping interests in Savannah. He likely wooed them with the idea that the first steamship should sail from their port, then one of America's most prominent. He was soon rewarded. The Savannah

Steam Ship Company was formed to support this endeavor.

Rogers supervised the building of the ship carefully. It is said that he passed on every piece of machinery himself. Daniel Dod of Elizabeth, formerly of Mendham, New Jersey, was to design the engine based on a patent he held. James P. Allaire, whose iron works was formerly owned by Robert Fulton, was to cast the huge cylinder, one of the largest made up to that time. What a revolutionary ship she was for her times: a sailing vessel with an auxiliary steam engine that operated paddle wheels! When the weather was unfavorable for sails, the engine could take over the job.[62]

The Steamship Savannah Monument plaques on the wall recognizing ships of importance named *Savannah*.

THE RIVER STREET MONUMENTS

Front view of the Steamship Savannah Monument.

The *Savannah* left New York on March 28, and arrived in Savannah on April 26, 1819. The ship caused quite a stir. Even President James Monroe with Secretary of War John C. Calhoun came to see this new thing and were given a cruise to see how she worked.

At first, it was impossible to assemble a crew. No doubt both potential passengers and crew noted the heavy, black coal smoke emitted from the stack and feared the sparks from the soft pine wood used to start the boilers. Most sailors had heard the nickname "steam coffin." Some believed that the paddle wheels would be hazardous in a storm, even if lashed to the deck; others feared the engine would break loose. In the end,

Stevens Rogers, sailing master and first officer (no blood relation to Moses, but later a brother-in-law) had to find a crew in New London, Connecticut, where he and the Captain had been born and were trusted.[63]

The *Savannah* left for Liverpool, England, on May 22nd. She arrived there on June 20, and went from there to Stockholm and St. Petersburg, leaving there for her home port on October 10. When the voyage across the Atlantic Ocean began, Moses Rogers was eager to see the first European reaction. He was not disappointed. Off the coast of Ireland, an attendant at a signal station spotted the *Savannah* and immediately assumed she was on fire. It took the *Kite*, a speedy British revenue cutter, four or five hours before she caught up to the *Savannah*. The captain of the *Kite* was slightly embarrassed when he was shown that his "rescue" was not needed. The newspapers told the story to the delight of their readers. The most amusing part of the incident was not revealed until years later; the only way the *Kite* could stop the *Savannah* was by firing warning shots across her stern.[64]

The SS *Steamship Savannah* caused quite a stir and is recognized every year when maritime communities in the United States celebrate National Maritime Day on May 22, the day the *Savannah* left to cross the Atlantic Ocean. It showed the possibility that steam-powered ships could indeed replace sail ships for transportation. The *Savannah* has also been honored when the first nuclear-powered cargo-passenger, supported by the United

Side view of the Steamship Savannah Monument. The paddle wheels were retractable, so when sails were in use, they would not drag in the water.

States government, with its own nuclear reactor at a cost of 46.9 million dollars, was built. It was launched on July 21, 1959, and called the NS *Savannah*.[65] Savannah has not only been a great port city, she has contributed to maritime technology and lore through the years.

Anchor Monument:
A Bon Voyage to our Sailor Friends

It has been said that in many ways Savannah's history is the history of its port. Thus, Savannah has always appreciated the sailors who come from all over the world to deliver and export supplies. Today, sailors from fifty-eight nations, as well as nearly 3,000 vessels, call on the Port of Savannah annually. Savannah's gratitude for these merchant marines has been and still is overseen by Florence Martus, who for forty-four years greeted and waved goodbye to every ship coming through the port. (For more on Martus, see the *Waving Girl* chapter.) Savannah's appreciation can also be seen at the historic Laurel Grove Cemetery's Sailors Burial Ground, hallowed to the "men who go down to the sea in ships and occupy their business in great waters," where ship captains and seamen from many lands—America, Norway, Sweden, England, Scotland, Ireland, and Germany—are interred. The lot was purchased, in 1860, by John Cunningham, a public-spirited citizen of Savannah, as a burial place for seafarers "who may die in this Port." A commemorative service for the officers and men of the merchant marine is held annually at this site on the Sunday nearest National Maritime Day, May 22, which is the anniversary of the departure of the "Steamship Savannah."

The Anchor Monument was erected by the Savannah Chapter of the Women's Propeller Club of the United States in 1974. The anchor sits atop a rectangular base composed of four marble slabs, and lies in a small pool of water. The Monument was placed on River Street to remind people of the sailors all over the world who come to Savannah, and, for a brief while, call Savannah home. Some who die in this port far from their homes of origin end up resting here and become a part of who we are.

The Anchor Monument in honor of all sailors who have lost their lives at sea.

Anchor Monument.

The Liberty Ship Marker:
Give Me Liberty

The Sons of Liberty were started in Boston. They were responsible for the Boston Tea Party and were initiated to protect the rights of the colonists and to take to the streets against the taxes ordered by the British government. They were the precursors of resistance before the American Revolution. Every colony would eventually develop a group. In Savannah, they were a group of men who met at Tondee's Tavern to talk politics and plan for the independence of America. Tondee's Tavern would become the place of the first raising of the Liberty Pole and the first reading of the Declaration of Independence in Georgia. Georgia did not send anyone to the first Continental Congress, but the Sons of Liberty met and began to foment revolution against British control.

After word of the battles at Lexington and Concord spread to Georgia, the Sons of Liberty and other Georgians became more radical to the colonist cause against Britain. The Sons of Liberty broke into the powder magazine in Savannah on May 11, 1775, and divided the powder with their fellow South Carolina revolutionaries. In June, they learned of a ship that was carrying even more gunpowder to Savannah. On July 4, 1775, a second now more aggressive Georgia Provincial Congress met. They convened at Tondee's Tavern and voted to join the Continental Congress, allying themselves with the other colonies.

They also commissioned the first American naval vessel, a schooner called *Liberty*. The confiscated schooner was

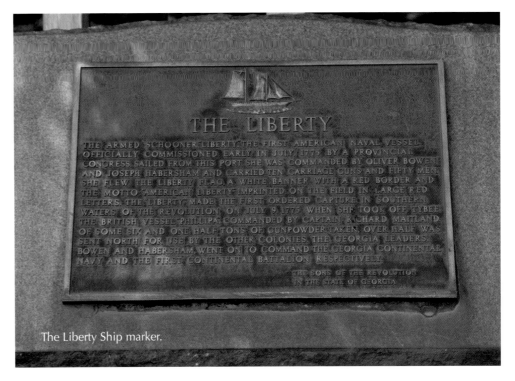

The Liberty Ship marker.

the property of the Royal Provincial Governor James Wright. After securing the schooner, they enlisted Oliver Brown of South Carolina and Savannahian Joseph Habersham to captain it.[66] The first action of the boat was to join the two South Carolina barges in the Savannah River set up to prevent the delivery of gunpowder to Savannah. On July 8th, two ships were seen anchored off the coast. They had previously been alerted that a ship carrying gunpowder was coming to Savannah. One of these ships was called the *Phillipa* and it was indeed carrying gunpowder to Savannah. As *Phillippa* moved upriver, the captain got a closer look at the schooner. "The schooner was full of armed men and had ten carriage-guns mounted."

The "*Liberty* fired two muskets at the *Phillippa* as a signal to pull aside. The *Phillipa* made one futile effort to escape before it had to surrender. The captain of the *Phillipa* demanded to know who had the audacity to attack them. They proclaimed their schooner's name was the *Liberty*.[67]

Four thousand of the 16,000 pounds of gunpowder taken off the *Phillipa* were delivered to the Continental Congress in Philadelphia. The Revolution had started in Georgia. All the names of the Georgia Sons of Liberty are not known because of their secrecy, but at least two of the names we do know: Edward Telfair and Dr. Noble W. Jones. Today, these men and their ship, the *Liberty*, are not always the first names we think of when we talk about the American Revolution, but the men were as deeply invested in the forming of a new nation as anyone else, and the ship was the first in what would one day become the greatest navy in the world.

Peace Pole in Morrell Park: All We Are Saying Is Give Peace a Chance
Tucked near the east end of River Street is Morrell Park, a small stretch of green space. In the middle of the southern part of the park is a simple three-foot wooden obelisk with words on all four sides. This

Neglected Peace Pole in Morrell Park.

is Savannah's Peace Pole. It has the words "May Peace Prevail On Earth" written in four languages and is a prayer and dream for the world. There are over 200,000 peace poles located across the globe. These poles are reminders for people to work to bring world peace.

The pole in Savannah was brought into being by some local peace activists. From time to time, different activities are held here. But if you look closely at the pole, you will find the bottom by the ground being whittled away by a weed whacker and the four languages on faded surfaces behind Plexiglas. It would give the impression that peace is having a hard time in today's world. But the pole seems appropriate, so close to the *Waving Girl*, who is welcoming the world to Savannah's harbor and the Olympic Cauldron representing a time when nations were more interested in being together competing in sports games than in politics and war. And we all know a prayer for peace in the world could not hurt.

Lion's Club Monument: We Serve
"We Serve" is a simple motto. It came from a Chicago insurance agent named Melvin Jones. He was invited to join a club in downtown Chicago called the Business Circle. The Business Circle was composed of leaders in the fields of trade and commerce. If it *had* a motto, in those days it would be: "You scratch my back and I'll scratch yours." The purpose was business. The members patronized each other, boosted each other's services or products, and met solely for the purpose of advancing their own interests.

Local Lion's Club Monument.

In his work as secretary of the Circle, Jones began to feel uneasy and that something was wrong with the picture. The club had potential to do so much good for their communities, but was organized only to help each other. They met, dined, and congratulated themselves and often profited through the contacts they made there. The very same things were happening in other cities as groups of businessmen met. Why, asked Melvin Jones, couldn't this selfish group power be directed to unselfish service in other areas of community life? "What if these men who are successful because of their drive, intelligence, and ambition, were to put their talents to work improving their communities?" Jones's personal code was, "You can't get very far until you start doing something for somebody else."[68]

With these thoughts, Jones, in 1917, began a journey that today culminates

The foundation around the flagpole of the Lion's Club Monument. The acronym "LIBERTY, INTELLIGENCE, OUR NATION'S SAFETY" [LIONS] is the local club's motto.

in the Lions Clubs International (LCI) a secular service organization with over 45,500 clubs and more than 1,368,683 members in 205 countries around the world. These clubs have helped 8,000,000 people with cataract surgeries; $6,000,000 has been raised for earthquake victims; 41,000,000 children and adults have been vaccinated for measles to list a few of their achievements.

The local chapter of the Lion's Club was chartered in 1922. They chose as their slogan an acronym of the word Lions (Liberty, Intelligence, Our Nation's Safety). This is found at the base of the flag pole. The local chapter supports sight conservation through the Lighthouse Foundation, Georgia Camp for the Blind, and the Project Vision program. They have offered glasses to those who could not afford them in the community for years. This memorial reminds us that the Lions Club is here improving the world by living out a simple motto "We Serve."

Waving Girl Monument: So Glad to See You

Florence Martus was, in many ways, an unlikely candidate for recognition and yet she earned one of the more significant monuments in Savannah for her welcoming heart and a sense of civic duty. She was the daughter of a lighthouse keeper living on Elba Island at the mouth of the Savannah River. She grew up in an isolated existence on this island watching the ships go by. When her father died, her brother was named the new lighthouse keeper and she went to live with him—on the island once

again. One day, as a teenager, she took it upon herself to welcome all the ships that came in the harbor by waving a towel and waving it again as they left. It was a simple act of a young woman who probably liked to hear the whistles of the ships recognizing her as they passed. But it was no momentary fancy; from 1887 to 1931, for forty-four years she would welcome and wish goodbye to every ship that came to the Savannah Harbor without missing a day. As the years went by and the sailors talked, they looked forward to the waving girl who welcomed them. They would bring her mementos and other gifts. At least once during hurricane winds, she and her brother heard the cries of a troubled ship and they took to their sturdy rowboat to rescue the passengers. She became, for the sailors of the world, a symbol of welcome and safe harbor.

As her legend grew, stories about her took on more fanciful forms. One of the most popular stories was that she greeted the ships because a sailor she loved had promised to return one day. (This story has a particular resonance with men who love to think women spend their time pining for them.) So, at each ship, she waved in the hopes that it would be the one carrying her long-lost lover. A pleasant enough thought, she once admitted, but far from the simple truth. "That's a nice story. But what got me started... I was young and it was sort of lonely on the island for a girl. At first I would run out to wave at my friends passing, and I was so tickled when they blew the whistle back at me."[69] Her family wanted to protect her from the

THE RIVER STREET MONUMENTS

The Waving Girl Monument.

legend; they refused Savannah-native television and film star Stacy Keach the rights to her story because they thought Hollywood would emphasize the legend.

On her seventieth birthday, the city of Savannah gave her a party in recognition of her life as Savannah's maritime goodwill ambassador. She called it the grandest day of her life. Bands played and politicians speechified. She would die five years later. After she passed away, sailors would ask about her and, truly, Savannah's harbor did not seem the same. Seven months after her death, one of Savannah's famed

Liberty Ships was christened with her name: the SS *Florence Martus*. Later, the Altrusa Club decided to build a monument to her that would stand as an eternal welcome to the sailors who passed through Savannah's harbor. The monument is the first memorial of a Georgia woman in any city park.

At first the monument was to be built on Washington Square in the Historic District, adjacent to the square with the Seamen's House. The International Seamen's House is an organization started by the Savannah Port Society aiding sailors in their

legal, recreational, and religious needs; the Society was organized in 1843. This was thought to be an appropriate location for the Martus memorial. Two things then occurred: the site was found inadequate to hold a monument of any size and the money-raising was found to be formidable. The Altrusa Club did not know what to do. It was at this time a similar thing happened as that in the Confederate Memorial: a prominent businessman stepped in to help with the project. Mills B. Lane Sr. was a Savannah banker and philanthropist who was intrigued with the monument. He said he would ensure the monument was finished on two conditions: the statue was to be in bronze and the sculptor the committee had wanted, but decided they could not afford, was to be hired. They agreed; Lane called sculptor Felix de Weldon and the work began.

Felix de Weldon was one of the most prominent sculptors of the day. He is the only sculptor to have a monument on all seven continents. In Antarctica, he has a statue of Admiral Richard Byrd, the famous explorer who some credit with finding the North Pole. He also has a bust of Elvis Presley in that uncharted continent of Graceland. De Weldon was the President of the American Institute of Architecture and his most famous sculpture is in Washington, DC; the statue of Marines lifting the flag at Iwo Jima.

Lane had made preliminary drawings of how the statue should look; de Weldon following the basic concept. Savannahians, a little wiser after being "surprised by the final product of other monuments, such as the Greene and Confederate monuments, had a mock-up presented to the public before the casting of the statue. There were only two changes. De Weldon sculpted her barefoot, but her family and friends said she was too much of a lady to be barefoot. So the actual shoes she wore were found and shipped to de Weldon. The other was the breed of dog was changed to Martus' collie. The statue was placed on the bluff of the Savannah River on River Street. It stands seventeen feet tall; Martus is waving a towel and her trusty dog stands beside her; on the ground sits a lantern that she would have used at night. The base is a polished-black, Swedish granite, eleven feet square. The captain who brought the statue to Savannah refused pay because he remembered fondly the waving girl who had welcomed him.[70]

The woman who for forty four years waved at passing ships stands ready to welcome ships once again from all over the world. It is also apropos that the only sculptor who has work all over the world is her immortalizer. The welcome and safe harbor to the Port of Savannah has returned and will never leave.

Olympic Torch Monument: A Sailing We Will Go

In 1996, the Olympics came to Atlanta, Georgia. Muhammad Ali lit the Olympic Torch, Iggy the computer-animated mascot came into being, the Olympic bomber set off an explosive in Olympic Centennial Park, and the world was focused on Atlanta for two weeks.

Savannah, to a smaller degree, was able to share in the Olympics. The Olympic Torch passed through Savannah on its way to Atlanta, and the Olympic Regatta was held here. This felt very appropriate since one of Atlanta's most famous media magnates and

The Waving Girl with her dog and lantern to wave at ships during the night.

The Waving Girl from behind shows her gesturing at a passing ferry boat.

The Olympic Torch was forged here in Savannah by blacksmith Ivan Bailey at the time of the 1996 Olympics.

sailors first learned to sail in Savannah at the age of eleven: Ted Turner.

The Marriott Hotel on River Street became the Olympic Village; seventy-seven countries with 682 athletes took part in the Regatta. On Monday, July 8, 1996, the official Olympic flag was unfurled on the second floor balcony of City Hall, where it hung throughout the Olympic Games. Mayor Floyd Adams Jr. was joined by County Commission Chairman Joe Mahany and mayors of several other Chatham County municipalities for the ceremony. The following day, the Olympic Torch arrived in Savannah on River Street. Thousands of spectators lined the streets as it made its way to Forsyth Park, before setting out across Chatham County and the state towards Atlanta and the opening ceremony there on July 19, 1996.

Because Savannah was so far removed from Atlanta, it was decided that the city should hold its own opening and closing ceremonies. The Olympic Torch in Morrell Park was lit with the original flame from Athens, Greece. The Savannah Olympic Support Council, SOSCO, a non-profit organization, raised $1.2 million for the Opening and Closing Ceremonies in Savannah. The famed anchorman Walter Cronkite was the host for the events. Ray Charles performed a free concert originally planned for Forsyth Park, but after the Atlanta bombing, it was moved to the Civic Center. Savannah hosted sixty cultural events in a 100-day festival running from May 1st through August 8, 1996. Specific events included a King Oliver Jazz Festival (the famed

mentor of Louis Armstrong, who died in Savannah), a homage to noted lyricist and Savannah native Johnny Mercer, and exhibitions, theater programs, and dance performances. A "Sounds of Savannah" program had musicians performing in the squares and parks. As a festival-ending event, everyone who performed in the "Sounds of Savannah" came together in a grand finale concert featuring the Savannah Symphony. The Closing Ceremonies ended at Morrell Park with fireworks over the Savannah River, accompanied by the lyrics of Ray Charles' *Georgia On My Mind*.

One of Savannah's own sailors competed in the regatta: John Porter III. Four countries won their first-ever yachting medals in Savannah: Hong Kong, Japan, Poland, and the Ukraine. It was a heady and celebrative time for the city. One of the big challenges was Savannah's geography. A marina was erected in Wassaw Sound by connecting twenty-seven barges built four miles out into the ocean.

Standing in the middle of the Opening and Closing Ceremonies was the Olympic Torch Monument. Ivan Bailey, an artist who had lived in Savannah from 1973 to 1982 until he moved to Atlanta, designed the monument. Bailey received a Master of Fine Arts from the University of Georgia and later won a fellowship to learn forging at an art school in Aachen, Germany. In 1973, he established Bailey's Forge on Bay Street. His ironwork can be found throughout Savannah. His works include the Sunflower Gate at 345 Habersham Street, fountains at historic buildings such as the King Tisdell Cottage, the Isaiah Davenport House, and the bed and breakfast inn at the Eliza Thompson House.[71] Bailey described the Olympic Torch Monument this way: "Those years [of living in Savannah] gave me an insight into the kind of work the people would take unto themselves and therefore it is a fairly straightforward, somewhat classical sculpture. Savannahians are somewhat distant from the cutting edge. Besides, this was a piece that should transcend the style of the moment and be a permanent part of a city with tons of heritage."[72]

Bailey writes on his website:

The columns are based upon both several other works I did in Savannah and especially, with the tie-in to the 100-year anniversary of the modern games in mind. They are especially inspired by the columns of the Porch of The Maidens on the Acropolis in Athens. The six lovely Greek maidens holding up the roof have been a favorite of mine since art history days in college. I chose five rather than six columns both because this is a lesser work, but also and primarily because I have always loved asymmetry. The visual effect of five rather than four or six, is remarkable and seldom to be seen. The five-sided capitals resemble the heads and the waist, fluted columns suggest the "chiton" or dresses the maidens are wearing. The original design spaced the

Close-up of the sails and fire of the Olympic Torch.

columns widely apart, each with a sail on top and a lower cauldron in the center. The Arts Ashore group felt that a taller compact design would be more effective. In retrospect, considering the site, I cannot strenuously disagree. The plinth, or pancake as I referred to it during construction, brought the piece closer to the Maidens Porch effect. The six sails are obviously a celebration of the purpose of the venue. The fire bowl, open at the top during the games would be surmounted by a copper flame afterward. The direction the flame will point to will be determined by the direction of the wind at the time of the opening ceremonies.[73]

The Olympic Torch Monument stands today as a testament to a period when the world's sailing community had all eyes on Savannah. Savannah had proven itself as capable of hosting an event of international importance. This would be the beginning of many other events, such as the Savannah Music Festival, the Liberty Mutual Heritage Golf Tournament, the Savannah Film Festival, and the G-8 summit media headquarters. Just as the neighboring statue of the *Waving Girl* welcomed the world's "business sailors," we welcomed the world's "sports sailors" to our port. It acts as witness to the Olympic hope that every port of the world will always be welcoming and the world will be a place of peace.

Desoto Monument: We Should Have Done Better by You

This monument hearkens back to the first contact of two cultures: the Native American and Spanish. Yes, before British General James Oglethorpe came Spanish explorer Hernando Desoto. On March 3, 1540, Desoto left Florida and explored the region of Georgia. By September 5, 1540, he had left and continued west, where he and many of his soldiers would die. Desoto was the first European to explore the interior of what is now the United States. He had previously participated in the capture of Panama and Nicaragua and also played a significant role in the defeat of the Incas in Peru. He was a great explorer who sought title, fame, and fortune.

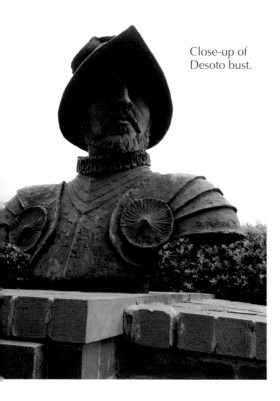

Close-up of
Desoto bust.

Hernando Desoto Monument, the first European to explore Georgia.

Desoto and his men were ruthless in their dealings with the Native Americans, often as the instigator of battles between the two. They also brought illness. The Europeans, who had lived in heavily populated communities, had built immunity to many diseases. The Native Americans who had lived in smaller communities and had less contact with a variety of people had not built immunity to many of these human illnesses. The Spanish also insisted on proselytizing their Catholicism, many times at the point of a gun.

This monument marks 500 years since Catholics and Jews came to settle in America in 1492. It is a different age now and the local Armstrong Atlantic State University (AASU) Hispanic Society commissioned and erected this monument. AASU alumnus and local thespian Billy Nelson was the sculptor. The monument appropriately sits on the riverside terrace of Savannah's downtown Marriott Hotel, which was the site of Savannah's Olympic Village for the Olympic sailing competition in 1996.

It has a very Olympic message on the plaque:

Acknowledging error and truth we dedicate this monument to an era of diverse religious and social consciousness in our history hoping to generate a new faith in the renewed quest for universal justice and peace among people of all races and creeds."

This simple monument holds huge truths for us.

III
THE
BAY STREET
MONUMENTS

Old Harbor Light.

Old Harbor Light:
A Shining Light in the Midst of the Wrecks We Have Made

On the bluff at the eastern end of Emmett Park, standing twenty-five to thirty feet high, is what originally was referred to as the Beacon Range Light. It stands approximately seventy-seven feet above the Savannah River and originally had a red light that directed night ship traffic past "The Wrecks." The Wrecks were six vessels that were sunk by the British in the channel. The British were hoping to impede French and American ships from using the port by creating a shipping hazard for their vessels. The light was erected later by the United States Lighthouse Board in 1858.

In 1932, it was called Old Harbor Light by a Chicago journalist writing for the *Savannah Herald and Examiner*. The name stuck, although it was a misnomer of its purpose. The light became even more endearing to Savannahians when Charleston Renaissance artist Elizabeth O'Neill Verner's painting of it was published in the *Savannah Morning News* in 1926. Verner was widely recognized as the matriarch of the Charleston Renaissance. She was known for her depictions of colorful flower sellers, coastal landscapes, and the streets and alleyways of Charleston. Verner became the aesthetic voice of the Southern Coastal area. She promoted the beauty of the Coast through her teaching, lecturing, and four books illustrated with her etchings.

She also illustrated DuBose Heyward's *Porgy and Bess*. Her work is found in the collections of the Boston Museum of Fine Arts, the Metropolitan Museum of Art, the Harvard Museums of Art, as well as Charleston's Gibbes Museum of Art, and many other Southern art institutions.[74] She created images of her native city that would captivate the imaginations and heart of many with her works that defined the culture of Charleston and the Low Country. She was a charter member of the Preservation Society of

Old Harbor Light surrounded by landscaped park and various anchors.

Charleston, helping to inspire similar efforts in Fayetteville, North Carolina, and Savannah, Georgia. So it is no surprise her painting of the Old Harbor Light caught the hearts of Savannahians and created a quintessential image of the South.

Even though the light was turned off during World War II for security reasons and slowly deteriorated for years, it was never removed. In 2001, the Savannah Garden Club and the city of Savannah made the area surrounding the light into a park and restored it to its old grandeur. Today, it stands surrounded by a landscaped park along with anchors from various ships. If one looks closely for a moment you may catch a spirit of a proud Southern Heritage.

Noble Wimberly Jones Bust: Morning Star of the Revolution

We have all heard of the *Mayflower,* but for Georgians it was the good ship *Anne.* The *Anne* brought General James Oglethorpe and the first European settlers to Georgia on February 1, 1733. On that ship was one of the most prominent of Georgia immigrants: Noble Wimberly Jones, who was only thirteen at the time. His father, Noble Jones, paid his own passage and those who did not come as indentured servants were given civic offices and land grants. His father fought with General Oglethorpe in the Siege of Augustine against the Spanish and, in August 1740, was sent to watch the Narrows of Skidaway Island. He was commissioned to the rank of lieutenant, later captain, by General Oglethorpe. He was also very active in the Crown's politics and would remain a Loyalist throughout his life. Jones would perform a variety of roles in the new colony of Georgia including: constable, physician, surveyor, Indian agent, soldier, member of the Royal Council, treasurer, and Senior Justice of the Province. In 1736, Jones leased 500

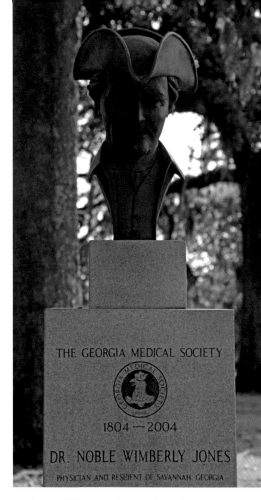

Dr. Noble Wimberly Jones's bust sits on top of Georgia Medical Society's monument celebrating its 200th anniversary.

acres from the Trustees of Georgia and, in 1745, finished construction of the fortified home he named "Wormslow." (Originally spelled "Wormslow," it is now usually spelled "Wormsloe.")

From this outpost, Jones commanded a company of marines charged with patrolling the inland water route and alerting Savannah of any Spanish attack. Noble Jones, the father, served as a physician for the colonists after Dr. William Cox, an Englishman, died of consumption Cox had been the ship's surgeon on the *Anne*; Noble Jones had watched and assisted him during the crossing—such was the extent of his medical training. The remains of the plantation and fort are found in Wormsloe State Park on the Isle of Hope. At the entrance of the park is an arch over the road with the words "Wormsloe" etched on it. The road leading to the plantation is flanked by rows of oak

Close-up of Dr. Noble Wimberly Jones's bust.

trees that run for one and a half miles. Some of the descendants continue to live on this plantation today.

As was common in those times, Noble Wimberly Jones served an apprenticeship under his father and became a physician. Noble Wimberly Jones was the father of the businessman who rescued the Confederate Monument Project for the United Daughters of the Confederacy, George Wimberly Jones Derenne. Unlike his father, Noble W. Jones was called the "Morning Star of the Revolution" and was one of the major American Revolutionary War heroes. Noble Jones the father remained a Tory and loyal to the Crown. Noble W. Jones (the son) was prominent among Georgia's Whig leaders and was one of the Savannah Sons of Liberty. In May 1775, news of the shot heard around the world in Massachusetts electrified Georgia's Whigs; Jones and several other revolutionaries, including Joseph Habersham, John Milledge, and Edward Telfair, broke into Savannah's royal magazine. They seized 600 pounds of gunpowder and sent some to the rebels in Boston. The next Georgia Provincial Congress met in July 1775 and elected Jones a delegate to the Continental Congress. However, his father's terminal illness kept him in Savannah, where, by year's end, he was serving on the Revolutionary Council of Safety. Obviously, the tension between the patriot and the loyalist did not outweigh the love and familial responsibility between the two.

Noble W. Jones was a member of the convention that created the state's constitution of 1777. The British captured Savannah in 1778, forcing Jones to escape to Charleston, South Carolina. He was captured when the city fell to the British in 1780. Jones was finally freed through a 1781 prisoner exchange. He was released to Philadelphia, Pennsylvania, where he served as a Georgia delegate to the Continental Congress. While there he practiced medicine under the tutelage of Benjamin Rush, a signer of the Declaration of Independence and considered the father of American psychiatry.

Jones returned to Savannah in 1788. In 1795, he presided over the convention that met to amend the Georgia Constitution in 1789. In 1804, after having retired from politics, he helped organize the Georgia Medical Society and became its first president. Jones would practice medicine until his death in 1805. As the last connection to the original Savannah settlers and a celebrated patriot who was a leader in the colony's struggle for independence from Britain his death was mourned citywide.[75]

The bust in honor of Noble Wimberly Jones was to commemorate the 200th anniversary of the Georgia Medical Society. The Georgia Medical Society of Savannah is the oldest local Medical Society in the United States. The Society constituted on December 12, 1804, and has been an active county medical society since that date. The Society consists of physicians practicing in the counties of Chatham, Effingham, Bryan, McIntosh, and Long counties. The contributions of this group to Georgia are enumerated on the sides of the monument.

The sculptor was Kevin Conlon, who has been working as a professional artist for over twenty years. Some of his works include a portrait of Teh-he Li, now installed at Aletheia University's Matou campus in Taiwan; a portrait of Julie Backus-Smith, a former Chatham County Commissioner for the First District, installed at Bonaventure Cemetery in Savannah, Georgia; as well as a portrait of the golfer, Sam Snead, installed at the Club at Savannah Harbor.[76]

It is said that Noble Jones was the only original settler of Georgia who stayed in the colony. If anyone embodied the vision of James Oglethorpe, to give people a second chance to use their talents to build a new world, it would be the Jones family and Noble W. Jones would especially exemplify this vision.

Chatham Artillery Monument: One for the Road

Savannah is known for being a military town. The presence of Hunter Army Airfield, Fort Stewart nearby, and the founding of the Mighty Eighth Air Force here bolster that identity. So it is no surprise that the Chatham Artillery Company, organized May 1, 1786, by Edward Lloyd, a one-armed veteran of the Revolutionary War, is the second oldest military organization in the United States. Its first important duty was the military burial of General Nathanael Greene here in Savannah. The Artillery has participated in almost every American war since its founding. The Oconee Wars, War of 1812, Mexican War (called up but not used), Civil War (on the Confederate's side), Spanish-

American War, World Wars I and II, Korean War, Vietnam War, Gulf War, and the Iraq War to list a few. They have also performed military duties, such as the welcoming of George Washington to Savannah with a twenty-six gun salute and they have served as the honor guard of the Marquis de Lafayette in 1825 during his tour of America. Today, the force is no longer called the Chatham Artillery but has morphed into the First Battalion of the 118th of the Field Artillery Regiment of the Georgia National Guard.

The monument's total height is eleven feet. It was dedicated May 1986, on the Artillery's 200th birthday. The design was inspired by and is quite similar to the 101st Airborne Memorial in Arlington National Cemetery. On the front is inscribed:

> To honor the members of the Chatham Artillery Servants of God, Country, State and Community. Soldiers in War Patriots in Peace.

Its long and distinguished military history is a source of pride for Savannahians. But the Chatham Artillery's name has also been used as a source of pride of another kind. Soldiers who face death often seek to grab life with all their vigor while at play. So it is said that, in the mid nineteenth century, an all-volunteer Savannah regiment called the Republican Blues, organized in 1808, visited Macon. The Chatham Artillery unit, seizing any reason for a party, greeted the Blues with a hardy welcome and a little gift. The gift was to

---

CHATHAM ARTILLERY PUNCH

Serves 100 People
(Or Ten Admirals)
Makes 5 gallons

Ingredients
1 ½ gallons Catawba Wine
1 ½ quarts Rye Whisky
½ gallon St. Croix Rum
½ pint Benedictine
1 quart Gin
1 quart Brandy
1 ½ gallons strong tea
2 ½ pounds brown sugar
Juice from 18 oranges
Juice from 18 lemons[77]

Directions
Mix 36-48 hours before serving. Add one case of champagne when ready to serve.

If you have a little time and nothing to do you might just try a little Chatham Artillery Punch. And if you are still standing, remember to thank the Chatham Artillery for their service both in war and play.

---

brew a new punch in honor of the Blues and thus the Chatham Artillery Punch was born. This punch would become notorious for its punch. It tasted good, but had a sly, shy kick. The punch is said to have knocked out Admiral Winfield Scott Schley when he visited Savannah in 1899 after the Spanish-American War. They claim Admiral Cervera's (of the Spanish Army in Cuba during the Spanish-American War) cannon shells were harmless to the brave American admiral, but Chatham Artillery Punch scored a direct hit, which put him out for two days.

Vietnam War Monument: A Long Way From Home

There is a wall in Washington, DC, that for many has become our modern-day Wailing Wall. When it was built, the critics were many, but time has made the design by Maya Lin, with the names of those who died etched in the somber, black granite, now praised. Since 1992, a smaller version has traveled throughout the United States for veterans and their families who cannot not make the journey to D.C.

The Savannah Vietnam War Memorial was dedicated on June 29, 1991. It may be the most expensive monument in Savannah. The monument was the concept of a Gulfstream Aviation designer, Matthew Dixon, the winner of a contest for best design. It honors the 106 soldiers killed or MIA and the over 25,000 survivors in Coastal Georgia. Jim Hudson, an artisan of Boone's Mill, made the peninsula.[78]

The creation of the monument was a grassroots effort started by a mother and her veteran son. The memorial, while not as stark or formal as the Vietnam Wall, is still thought-provoking. It is made out of white marble and this changes the tone. A reflecting pool surrounds the carved sculpture of Vietnam. In a corner is a marble slab etched with the names of the fallen. On top of the sculpted Vietnam is

Vietnam War Memorial from sidewalk next to Bay Street.

Map of Vietnam is shaped on top of granite.

A Vietnam soldier's burial site symbol: helmet, M-16, and boots.

a bronze grave marker, along with army boots, dog-tag, M-16 rifle, bayonet, and helmet. The tools of the soldier rest by the grave marker in a country we are divided from by both fence and the water in the reflecting pool. It is as though we sit here in America and see the war that is going on and cannot reach out to stop or comfort those who lost so much in a land far away.

Today, annual memorial services are held here by the survivors, families, friends, and others who wish to support those who have left the ghost of a soldier in a place many of us will never go.

Irish Monument:
Come Dance a Jig With Us

The Savannah Irish are well known. The Savannah St. Patrick's Day Parade is one of the four largest in the United States. Savannah's downtown has the mark of the Shamrock throughout the Historic District. There are Irish pubs, societies, a park named after an Irish hero, a Cathedral, and other Irish influences. Yet, when the Irish first came, there was a deep prejudice against them. Many of the Irish came as indentured servants. This was the only way many could afford to migrate to America. They were poor laborers without much social standing or education. In the 1740s, the Irish made up nine out of ten indentured servants in some colonial regions.[79] This made them one step above a slave. In fact, when the Irish first came to Savannah, they were housed in the same neighborhoods as the black community. Yet the Irish would rise because they could move wherever they chose after

70

their indenture ended. They did not have the ravages of slavery and skin color with which to deal. They were also able to choose locations, such as Savannah, where they might find support in family, friends, or community—and more importantly work. Over time this enabled them, as one book has commented, to become white.

Most Irish did not directly migrate to Savannah; they would enter via one of the northeast ports and, through talking with other Irish and reading the Irish newspapers started by these communities, they could determine where might be a better place to go. One of the indicators found in every paper were articles written about various St. Patrick's Day parades in America. Savannah had one of the earliest parades (1813 or 1824 depending on whom you ask).[80] The parade was in existence for at least twenty-four years before what was seen as the peak of the Irish immigration between 1848 and 1852. The mayor and other dignitaries participated in the parade. Also happening in 1850 was the beginning of the construction of the Central of Georgia Railroad. Because of the mixing of these things, people realized that work was available in Savannah. A perfect storm for what is called the Second Wave of Irish immigrants had been created. The Irish helped build this city with their hard labor, eventually becoming leaders in the

Irish Monument. This is a Celtic Cross. Notice the award-winning carving on the cross. Erin Go Bragh means Ireland forever.

TO AMERICANS OF IRISH DESCENT
PAST — PRESENT — FUTURE
ERIN GO BRAGH

Irish Monument.

community and giving Savannah one of its signature events: the St. Patrick's Day Parade.

The Celtic Cross was one of several ethnic monuments built celebrating Savannah's 250th-year anniversary. The Celtic Cross is made from limestone from the County of Roscommon, in West Ireland. Every year, during the St. Patrick's Day Festival, a wreath is laid on its pedestal. The monument was carved by Cathal Cregg, who received the "Apprentice Stone-Cutter of the Year Award" from the Bank of Ireland.[81]

Korean War Monument: Remembering the Forgotten

The entry into the Korean War for Savannah's 182 Marines of the Dog Company Marine Reserve Unit started with a parade. Following the Corps' Parris Island band, the Savannah Marines marched up Abercorn Street to Broughton Street, took a left onto Broughton, and stepped off for West Broad Street—now Martin Luther King

D COMPANY, 10TH INFANTRY BATTALION, USMCR
SAVANNAH, GEORGIA
1948-1950
UPON ACTIVATION ON 21 AUGUST 1950, 182 SAVANNAH
MARINES ANSWERED THEIR NATION'S CALL TO DUTY
DURING THE KOREAN WAR.
ALL OF THESE MARINES GAVE SOME
FIVE GAVE ALL
SEMPER FIDELIS

Plaque at the foot of the
Korean War Monument.

HUTCHINS, FLETCHER M. JR. (KIA)
JERNIGAN, BRUCE L. JR.
KELLERMAN, LAWRENCE R.
KENDRICK, LARRY C.
KENDRICK, MALCOLM E.
LANIER, ROBERT J.
LAWHON, JONATHAN H.
LIPTON, CHARLES J.
MACMILLAN, THOMAS H.
MANSON, MARION H.
MASSMAN, ALVIN L.
MATTINGLY, ALFRED B.
MATTOX, WILLIAM K.
MAYFIELD, JAMES H. (KIA)
McALEER, JAMES E. JR.
McCALL, CHARLES W. JR.
McCLURE, JOSEPH B.
McCORKLE, JAMES C.

Close-up of the names on the Korean War
Monument. The gold lettered names are
those who died in battle.

ABERNATHY, MOSES E.
ADAMS, JACK R.
ADKINS, HARRY L.
ALEXANDER, NORWARD M.
ANDERSON, CLYDE R.
ARNOLD, JOE A.
ARSENEAU, JOHN A.
BALDWIN, FREDERICK C.
BARBER, ROBERT L.
BARNES, NESBERT A.
BATES, ROBERT L. JR.
BEASLEY, CHARLES V.
BELL, CHARLES B.
BELL, CLARENCE D.
BLATNER, HOWARD L.
BOAEN, HARRY W.
BODAFORD, GEORGE E. JR.
BODAFORD, WILLIAM H.
BOUDREAU, EDWARD G.
BOWEN, JAMES C.L.
BRAUN, JAMES M.
BROWN, JAMES S.
BROWN, ROBERT F.
CAIL, ROBERT S.
CANNON, MICHAEL W.
CARTER, WILLIAM B.
CHESTER, GROVER C.
CLARKE, JOSEPH W.
COBURN, EDWARD J.
COHEN, ALBERT I.
COHEN, HENRI M.
COLE, JAMES W. JR.
CONNERS, JOSEPH L.
COOLIDGE, WILLIAM M.
CORBIN, NEAL D.
CORBIN, PHILLIP C.
CORLEY, THOMAS G. JR.
COURINGTON, ROY N.
COWART, EUGENE H.
COWART, HARRY C.
COWART, OLLIE N. B. JR.
DAILEY, ERNEST E.
DAILEY, JOSEPH A.
DAMPIER, JIMMIE G.
DAMPIER, MALCOLM M.
DARLING, LOUIS O.

Korean War Monument. The Monument memorializes
the soldiers of D Company, 10th Infantry Battalion,
USMCR who fought in the Korean War.

Jr Boulevard—where they turned left again and headed to the train station. That night touched Savannah Marine Jim McNear. "The streets were packed," he remembers. "The city and Parris Island really turned out for that parade."[82]

The Korean War, which has been labeled the "forgotten war" by some, was no parade. The war lasted three years: from June 25, 1950, to July 27, 1953. Approximately 33,667 soldiers died and 5.7 million served in this war. The war had the fourth largest number of combat deaths in all of America's wars.

This Monument recognizes these soldiers and their willingness to serve their country. Five Savannahians would die in this war; the others would leave a little of themselves back in Korea. *They* would never forget this forgotten war. Now that this monument, erected in 2006, is here, engraved with the names of those 182 marines, *we* should never forget, either.

Georgia Hussars Monument: Riders in the Storm

The Georgia Hussars, a cavalry unit, was organized on February 13, 1736, by General James Oglethorpe to patrol and guard the colony from infringements of land by the Spanish and Native Americans. The Hussars would fight in some of the more significant battles of Georgia. They fought with Oglethorpe at Bloody Marsh in 1742. This battle secured St. Simon's Island for the British and turned back the Spanish and their expansionist ideas. The Georgia Hussars would join with General Casimir Pulaski, the father of the American

Cannon to memorialize the Georgia Hussars.

cavalry, in the Battle of Savannah during the Revolutionary War on the colonists' side. Their ill-fated charge against the British forces at the Spring Hill Redoubt would be turned back, and Pulaski would be mortally wounded.

This cavalry unit would fight in the Mexican War, the Civil War (for the Confederacy), and in World War I as a mounted force until 1940. They would continue to serve in World War II, as well as the Korean and Vietnam Wars. The Unit was deactivated in 1978 and assigned to the Georgia Army National Guard. Today, the Georgia Hussars are a hereditary group for the descendants.

A closer look at the Georgia Hussar cannon.

The cannon that sits here was used in the Revolutionary War Battle of Savannah. This cavalry unit marked with distinction is now remembered by a small cannon. But the unit's deeds have played a big part in the United States' military history.

Salzburger Monument: Never Again

The United States has always been a haven for different groups seeking religious and political freedom, and Savannah is no exception to this. The Moravians, Jews, Irish, Chinese, and others, at various times, came to Savannah looking to start a new life away from political tyranny and religious persecution. The Salzburgers were one of these groups.

In 1731, Count Leopold von Firmian, the Catholic archbishop and prince of independent Salzburg, issued the Edict of Expulsion that forced 20,000 Protestants to leave their homeland. A majority of the refugees would settle in East Prussia and Holland.[83] King George II of England sympathized with the Salzburgers and offered them a place in his Georgia colony. About 300 Salzburgers, under the leadership of Pastors Johann Martin Boltzius and Israel Gronau, accepted the invitation.

The first group of Salzburgers sailed from England to Georgia in 1734, arriving in Savannah on March 12th. They settled about twenty-five miles upriver on Ebenezer Creek and developed the town of New Ebenezer, laid out in a manner similar to Savannah. By 1741, the town had grown to a population of 1,200. Their

Sazlburger Monument.

success could be seen in the fact that they built the first saw mill in Georgia on Ebenezer Creek in 1735 and the first orphanage at New Ebenezer two years later. The first rice and grist mill in Georgia was begun here in 1740, the residents organized the first Sunday School in 1734, constructed the first church of any denomination, and developed a successful silk industry in 1741.[84]

The church they established was called the Jerusalem Church, later known as the Jerusalem Evangelical Lutheran Church. Its first pastor was Martin Boltzius. They practiced the Protestant qualities of piety, modesty, independence, and work effort, as evidenced by their thriving community.

These same qualities made the Salzburgers separate themselves from the other parts of the colony.

The Revolutionary War brought British troops, who set up headquarters at New Ebenezer. The soldiers plundered their supplies, used the church as a hospital and its pews as firewood. When finally American troops retook Ebenezer in 1782, they named it the capital of Georgia for two weeks.

In 1731, the Catholic country of Salzburg issued the Edict of Expulsion. This Edict forced 20,000 Protestants to leave their homeland, causing them to abandoned their property and holdings. Most of the fleeing Salzburgers went to East Prussia and Holland. Today the church still proudly stands and is one of the oldest continuing congregations in the United States. Many descendants of the Salzburgers still live in Effingham and Chatham Counties.

Close-up of the engraving on the Salzburger Monument. This depicts the exiled Salzburgers leaving their homes in Austria.

The monument came about because of the visit an Austrian diplomat Alfred Winter made to Savannah. Upon hearing the plight of the Salzburgers and their successful re-establishment in Ebenezer, as well as his country's treatment of them, he proposed a monument to make amends. This resulted in the Salzburger Monument of Reconciliation. The Monument of Reconciliation was dedicated by the State of Salzburg, Austria, a predominantly Roman Catholic country, to the descendants of the Protestant Georgian Salzburgers. The monument is green serpentine stone from the homeland of the first Georgia Salzburgers: the Hohe Tauern region of Austria.[85] The human figures sculptured in the stone depict the people forced from their homes in Salzburg. The inscription reveals the story of these people: "Denied Their Religious Freedom, They Were Forced to Leave Their Homeland."

The Salzburger Monument sits in the small Salzburger Park.

Dr. Hans Katschthaler, then governor of the state of Salzburg, commissioned Anton Thuswaldner, a renowned Austrian sculptor, to chisel the figures of the exiles on the stone. The completed work of art was first displayed in May 1994, with a ceremony held in front of Christ Lutheran Church on the Salzach River in Salzburg, Austria. A delegation of the Georgia Salzburger Society was in attendance when Dr. Katschthaler and the people of Salzburg unveiled and dedicated the monument. It was said at that ceremony that the sculpture would be remembered as the monument to understanding, so that this would never happen again.[86]

On September 5, 1994, the Salzburger Monument of Reconciliation, after shipment from Austria, was unveiled and dedicated to the Georgia Salzburger Society and given to the city of Savannah. This was the first monument to be given to Savannah by a foreign government.

What is now Salzburger Park lies between Lincoln Avenue and Abercorn Street on Bay Street.

On the top of Ebenezer Church stands a weather vane in the shape of a swan. Legend records a statement made by Jan Hus, an early predecessor of Martin Luther, as he was about to be burned at the stake for his supposed heresy: "You may burn this goose, but out of these ashes will arise a swan."[87] The swan on the Ebenezer Church stands today as a reminder of the many challenges the Salzburgers and other immigrants faced and how, in the ashes of their lives, a swan was raised.

Old City Exchange Bell: The Bell Tolls For Thee

This bell, the oldest in Georgia, has rung a welcome for such figures as Presidents James Monroe, James Polk, Millard Fillmore, and political dignitaries, such as Henry Clay, Daniel Webster, and the

The Old City Exchange Bell sits in a replica of the tower on the City Exchange that once stood where City Hall is today.

Marquis de Lafayette. It has also rung at the deaths of many of America's heroes, has been the warning signal for fires, and the sound to mark the end of the day for the City Exchange workers. It stood in the tower overlooking Savannah at the end of Bull Street for over 100 years, the sound of its peal etched in the very psyche of Savannahians during this time.

The bell was imported from Amsterdam and hung in the steeple above the old City Exchange. Along with municipal offices, the City Exchange housed the Customs House, a post office, and newspaper offices. The purchase of the City Exchange building by the city to make way for the new City Hall, with its gleaming golden dome and built in 1906, caused its permanent removal. Yet the citizens of Savannah did not, or could not, let the bell disappear from their memories. After a few other temporary homes, the bell finally came to rest at its current location in 1957. A replica of the tower in which it stood was created and the bell placed within it. Although it no longer rings, the sound of a different time can be heard when one stands before it.

Cotton Exchange Griffin:
Let's Make a Deal

The terra-cotta griffin is part of the design of famed William Gibbons Preston, who was the architect of the Savannah Cotton Exchange Building behind it. They go together and are components of what has been called King Cotton's Palace.

Old City Exchange Bell.

The terra cotta griffin fountain stands in front of the Cotton Exchange on Bay Street. Cotton prices were set in the Exchange and in the surrounding areas slaves would be sold.

THE BAY STREET MONUMENTS

The Savannah Cotton Exchange was established in 1876 and made its permanent home on Bay Street in 1883. The Exchange was established to provide brokers of cotton planters a place to congregate and set the price of cotton exported to larger markets such as New York or London. In 1887, Savannah was the greatest cotton seaport on the Atlantic and second in the world. Over two million bales a year were exported from Savannah. Of course, this was a natural outcome of the work of Eli Whitney, in 1793, on the Savannah plantation Mulberry Grove in improving the cotton gin's ability to separate the cotton from the seed. Cotton had become a commodity that made fortunes in Savannah.

The Cotton Exchange floor was buzzing with traders determining the price of cotton for everyone. Factors Walk, named such because, as cotton was being transported on the road below, men (called "factors") were on the bridges above beginning the bidding for it on its way to warehouses before being shipped to Europe. So, *inside*, the exchange prices were being determined and, *outside*, on Factors Walk, bids were being made for the cotton. Business was booming.

To celebrate that business, Savannah hired the renowned Boston architect William Preston Gibbons. His buildings include the first bungalow, Mechanics Hall in Boston, the Rogers Building of the Massachusetts Institute of Technology, the Massachusetts Charitable Mechanics Association Building, Boston University School of Law on Ashburton Place, thirty or more buildings of the Massachusetts School for the Feeble Minded, and the State Industrial School for Girls in Lancaster, Pennsylvania.

The terra cotta griffin fountain.

A close-up of the fence surrounding the griffin fountain. This fence once surrounded the Wetter Estate, now demolished, in Savannah. The fence features various famous men. Here we have playwright William Shakespeare.

In the Historic District of Savannah his mark can be found in the Chatham County Courthouse, Savannah College of Art and Design's Poetter Hall (where the college started), the rebuilt Independent Presbyterian Church, as well as some of Savannah's finest homes. But first, in 1887, he built King Cotton's Palace. He was one of eleven architects who entered the contest to see who would build this palace. He placed massive, red oak doors weighing 450 pounds on the facade and used the style of Romanesque Revival architecture to make sure the building stood out and was remembered. The building's engineering was unique, as it was the first to stand above a used road. The fountain was constructed in 1889. The griffin had the body, tail, and back legs of a lion; the head and wings of an eagle; and an eagle's talons. Griffins are known for guarding treasure and priceless possessions. The pride of Savannah's economic prowess was on display.

The shame of Savannah's economic power could also be found here in earlier years, for this area is where slaves were sold. The fence around the fountain came from an antebellum home (Wetter Estate) that was torn down, with statesmen, poets, and philosophers engraved on it. In 1952, the Cotton Exchange closed its doors. Cotton was no longer king. The times were changing. The Chamber of Commerce would live here until 1974, when Solomon's Lodge No. 1 would take over. The fountain and building guard the memory of a bygone era that brought great wealth and pain, reminding us of the potentials of economies to improve or oppress and the power is in our hands to decide.

The Washington cannons underneath a pavilion. George Washington gave these cannons to the Chatham Artillery for their service.

Washington Guns: I Just Want to Say Thank You

In 1791, George Washington paid a visit to Savannah. He is known to have slept somewhere, but it is certain he visited Catherine Greene (wife of Nathanael Greene, head of Washington's southern army) on Mulberry Grove Plantation. Not only was she a friend, but Washington had danced with her on several occasions at the parties of his officers during brief respites from the battles of the Revolutionary War.

Washington gave speeches and commendations to several Savannahians. He was feted with a twenty-six-gun salute by the four-year old Chatham Artillery at one event and likely made friends with several of the volunteer soldiers. In fact, one of the organizers of the Chatham Artillery was Captain Edward Lloyd, who had lost his arm in the Battle of Savannah. It was a grand few days in Savannah.

A side view of the terra cotta fountain.

THE BAY STREET MONUMENTS

One of the two Washington cannons.

After his visit, Washington, with Savannah still on his mind, presented two cannons to the city in honor of the Chatham Artillery. The cannons would become, if you do not include Tomochichi's burial stones placed by Oglethorpe in Wright Square as many do, Savannah's first and most important monument. The two cannons had been used by the British at the Battle of Yorktown. The cannons were made in Britain and France. An inscription on the British 6 pounder states that it was "surrendered by the capitulation of York Town Oct. 19, 1781." The English cannon was cast in 1758, during the reign of George II and the royal insignia and motto of the Order of the Garter appear on its barrel. The French gun was manufactured at Strasburg in 1756. On its elaborately engraved barrel appears the coat of arms of Louis XIV: the sun, which was the emblem of that monarch, and a Latin inscription that Louis XIV first ordered to be placed on French cannons, meaning "Last Argument of Kings."

The Washington Guns have announced with pride a welcome to many distinguished visitors to Savannah, including James Monroe, the Marquis de Lafayette, James K. Polk, Millard Fillmore, Chester A. Arthur, Jefferson Davis, Grover Cleveland, William McKinley, William H. Taft, and Franklin D. Roosevelt. Savannahians would come to call the cannons George and Martha after our first president and first lady. They quickly became proud trophies of our city.

During the Civil War, the cannons were taken off display and buried beneath a local armory. They would not be dug up and returned to public view until 1872, when Union troops completely withdrew from Savannah. This was done to ensure that the cannons would stay in Savannah and not be whisked away by Yankee hands.

Today, the cannons sit beneath a roof to preserve them and to show those who pass by that Savannah was one of the first thirteen colonies that fought for our independence.

City Hall Fountain: Coming of Age
Savannah's economy was enjoying boom years in the latter part of the nineteenth century and early decades of the twentieth century until the Great Depression. Herman Myers, Savannah's first Jewish mayor, came into office in 1895, toward the beginning of the economic heyday, but he lost reelection against Peter Meldrim in 1897. He ran again in 1899 and would stay mayor until 1907 when he retired. Myers was determined to use the good economic timing of his tenure as mayor to bring Savannah into the twentieth century with gusto. Under his leadership, Savannah built its Grand Union Station, demolished for urban renewal, and the City Hall that still stands today as one of the city's most prominent buildings.

The city chose Hyman Witcover, one of its most prolific architects, to design the building. Witcover was the architect of the Bull Street Carnegie Library; being a mason himself, it was appropriate that he designed the Scottish Rite Temple; being a Jew, it was fitting that he designed the B'nai B'rith Synagogue, which is now the Savannah College of Art and Design

The City Hall Fountain.

economic and political power. The bronze fountain is modeled after Andrea del Verrocchio's Palazzo Vecchio, city hall, in Florence, Italy. Verrocchio was an Italian sculptor and painter, and also credited as being the teacher of Leonardo da Vinci.

The fountain is the work of the Spanish sculptor Fernando Miranda y Casellas, who immigrated to New York City, where he was a well-established artist. The dolphins reflect Savannah's connection with the ocean and the putto holds the seal of Savannah and a cornucopia. The fountain stands in the middle of the foyer where, if one looks up, it is possible to see the seven-story interior stain-glassed dome. It is an impressive sight meant to communicate the arrival of Savannah as a world class city.

Oglethorpe Bench: Get a Good Night's Sleep Because Tomorrow We Have a Lot of Work to Do

General James Edward Oglethorpe, the founder of Georgia, had arrived on the ship *Anne* and visited Charleston and Beaufort. He had recruited engineer William Bull, who would lay out the streets and squares of Savannah. He had met with the Mico of the Yamacraws, Tomochichi, to negotiate the site he had chosen for the city. The site had the benefits of being on a bluff and surrounded by swamps and marshes for the defense he would need against the Spanish. Here, at this spot, on February 1, 1733, Oglethorpe pitched his tent on the night before the work of creating a new colony would begin.

Student Center. City Hall was probably Witcover's finest effort. It features a domed roof that rises seventy feet into the air. It was originally made of copper, but was gilded in 1987 with sheets of twenty-three-karat gold leaf. It was one of the greatest city halls in the South. Witcover used the Renaissance Revival style calling to mind the great cities of Europe.

Inside the foyer of City Hall stands an impressive dolphin fountain. The Fountain was to be the symbol of Savannah's

A close-up of the City Hall Fountain. The fountain was designed to sit here in the seven story domed rotunda of City Hall. It was to represent the wealth and prestige of Savannah.

Thoughts about the city plan, the Spanish in the south, and this new friend Tomochichi, must have all been racing through his mind as he tried to catch a good night's sleep before beginning the work he had waited for so long to do. All of these things probably made sleep hard; if the excitement about this new adventure did not prevent his sleep, his new friends, the sand gnats, would have. (Sand gnats are ubiquitous creatures that are not visible to the eye that live in the sandy soil of Coastal Georgia. The gnats can leave small welts from their bites.)

In 1889, the Centennial of President George Washington's inauguration was celebrated nationwide. Out of the renewed interest in United States history, numerous patriotic and preservation societies were founded. In Savannah, the Daughters of the American Revolution, Daughters of the Confederacy, Sons of the Revolution, and the Colonial Dames had joined forces to commission a monument for Oglethorpe. It had been many years ago since the pitching of his tent had passed and history had been made, and it was well past time

to honor this man. But the money was not forthcoming for the groups, so the Colonial Dames, afraid that if they did not act, not only would no great monument be erected, but nothing at all would occur. They acted and had built this monument in 1906, four years before the famous Daniel Chester French monument was to be procured for Chippewa Square.

They chose as their designer one of the region's distinguished architects, Julian de Buryn Kops. He designed the historic "Black" Carnegie Library,

Oglethorpe Bench marking the place where General Oglethorpe first camped in Savannah. Notice the mosaic step leading to the bench.

Side view of the Oglethorpe Bench.

A close-up of the engraved words on the Oglethorpe Bench.

using the Prairie style of Frank Lloyd Wright, the only such example in a civic building. The Oglethorpe Bench is found in the small Yamacraw Bluff Park west of City Hall. The granite bench is curved with scrolled ends. One of the two steps leading up to the bench is oval and decorated with a mosaic.

Today, tourists take pictures on the bench that marks the beginning of the Colony of Georgia and founding of Savannah. A lot has happened since February 1733: wars, steamships, plaques, Girl Scouts, cotton gins, events that Oglethorpe could not imagine. But we can know, tourist or native, we share one thing that Oglethorpe wished he knew nothing about: sand gnats.

THE BAY STREET MONUMENTS

IV
OTHER
HISTORIC DISTRICT
MONUMENTS

Johnny Mercer Statue: I Am Just Waiting for My Huckleberry Friend John, "Johnny," Herndon Mercer, born November 18, 1909, and died June 25, 1976, was an American musical icon with the likes of the Gershwin brothers, Irving Berlin, and Leonard Bernstein. Mercer and his song "Moon River" captured the imagination of the world and was obviously influenced by his youth in Savannah. He came from one of the quintessential Savannah families: his great-grandfather was Confederate General Hugh Weedon Mercer and he was a direct descendant of American Revolutionary War General Hugh Mercer, a Scottish soldier-physician who died at the Battle of Princeton. The Mercer House in Savannah was built by General Hugh Weedon Mercer in 1860, It later became the home of Jim Williams, whose trial for murder was

the centerpiece of John Berendt's book *Midnight in the Garden of Good and Evil*, although neither the general nor Johnny ever lived there.

Mercer is best known as a lyricist, but he also composed music and was a popular singer, recording his own songs as well as those written by others. From the mid-1930s through the mid-1950s, many of the songs Mercer wrote and performed were among the most popular hits of the time. He wrote the lyrics to more than 1,500 songs, including ninety compositions for movies and six Broadway shows, such as *St. Louis Woman* and *Lil' Abner*. He had hit songs with Bing Crosby in the late 1930s, with Jo Stafford, and on his own, especially "Accentuate the Positive." On the radio he sang with Benny Goodman and had his own shows, including Johnny Mercer's Music Shop. A small

The statue of Johnny Mercer in Ellis Square. The statue was made from a picture of Mercer from the *New York Times*.

The Mercer statue has become a favorite tourist spot for picture taking.

list of his songs includes familiar works, such as:

"Blues in the Night"
"That Old Black Magic"
"One For My Baby"
"Come Rain or Come Shine"
     —all collaborations with
     Harold Arlen
"Lazy Bones"
"Skylark" with Hoagy Carmichael
"I'm an Old Cowhand"
"I Remember You"
"P.S. I Love You"
"Jeepers Creepers"

"You Must Have Been a Beautiful
     Baby"
"When a Woman Loves a Man"
"Too Marvelous for Words"
"Fools Rush In"

He received nineteen Academy Award nominations, and won four for the songs listed here:

"The Atchison"
"Topeka and The Santa Fe," from
     1946 with Harry Warren
"In the Cool, Cool, Cool of the
     Evening," also done with
     Hoagy Carmichael, in 1951
"Moon River," in 1961 with
     Henry Mancini
"Days of Wine and Roses," again
     with Mancini, in 1962

As president and cofounder of Capitol Records, Mercer was instrumental in the early recording careers of such musicians as Peggy Lee and Nat King Cole. He created the Songwriters Hall of Fame. It would be fair to say he was one of America's greatest and most influential lyricists and composers.

If any monument in Savannah could be called a total Savannah project, this is it. The sculptor, Susie Grantham Chisholm, was born and raised in Savannah, Georgia. Her father was an architect and her mother had a degree in interior design. Chisholm majored in graphic design at the University of Georgia. After graduation, she returned to Savannah, where she worked as a graphic designer. After taking a class in sculpting, she knew she had found her passion. Since that class, she has had many

The Mercer statue.

public commissions: the Columbus Public Library, Columbus, Georgia; a reading girl for the Live Oak Public Library, main branch, Savannah; in the Savannah Islands YMCA; Azle Memorial Library, Azle, Texas; Benson Sculpture Garden in Loveland, Colorado; Summerville, South Carolina; and Lake Mayer, Savannah. She was also commissioned by the Boston Tea Party Museum to create a statue of Samuel Adams.

This monument was commissioned by the Friends of Johnny Mercer, as part of the centennial celebration of his birth. Susie Chisholm sculpted a smiling likeness saying, "I wanted the personality, the fun

OTHER HISTORIC DISTRICT MONUMENTS

Johnny, the Johnny that Savannah knew."[88] The sculpture was based on a picture in the *New York Times*, and is found in Ellis Square, where activity and music from the nearby restaurants and nightclubs of the City Market area can be heard. On occasion, you might even hear a Mercer song being played. He stands there, gap-toothed, reading his paper as a native Savannahian who left to go to New York and Los Angeles to make his mark. His music can be heard around the world, but it is here in Savannah, his final resting place, where his music can literally be heard and felt in the ambience of the city.

He was buried in Bonaventure Cemetery, where his grave has proven to be a tourist attraction. By the grave sits a bench with the names of some of his more popular songs, an etching of Mercer, and these words: "Buddy I'm a kind of a poet and I've gotta lotta things to say." Those "lotta things" Mercer said will be in the ears of music lovers everywhere and in every time.

Haitian Monument:
We Are All In for Freedom

Savannah takes great pride in its Revolutionary War heritage. One of the unique qualities of the Battle of Savannah was the many different nationalities who fought on the colonist side and the contributions of men, money, and material that aided the eventual success of American independence. The French, Polish, Native Americans, African slaves, Haitians, Germans, Hessians, Austrians, Scots, Welsh, Irish, English, Swedish, and American and West Indian colonials all participated as individuals or whole units

The Haitian Monument depicts soldiers during the Battle of Savannah.

in this most culturally diverse battle of the war. In preparation for the Battle of Savannah, these varied forces were divided into three armies, all strategizing and planning to end the occupation of Savannah by British soldiers. This battle resulted in huge casualties. Two heroes of the colonial army, Casimir Pulaski and Sergeant Jasper, died in the ensuing battle, and the Haitians, in particular, distinguished themselves.

It is not an often-discussed topic that Haitians fought alongside us for our freedom. In the Battle of Savannah, Haiti's great liberator first received his baptism in war. Twelve-year-old Henri Christophe participated in this fight, later becoming a leader in the struggle for Haitian independence from French colonial rule. Young Christophe in fact was to become commander of the Haitian army and later King of Haiti; he

The drummer boy is a depiction of Henri Christophe, future king and liberator of Haiti, who, at age twelve, fought with the colonists in the Battle of Savannah.

The face on this monument is the president of the Haitian-American Society at the time of the erection of the monument.

The face on this monument is of a Haitian donor and actor.

was to be the second head of state in the Western Hemisphere to be of African heritage. There were 500 Haitians who came here as freedmen and fought in the Battle of Savannah. They battled with courage and their actions that day, on September 16, 1779, saved the lives of many Continental soldiers. As the British were repelling the American attacks and defeat for the colonists was at hand, the Haitians offered cover to the other retreating American troops, preventing even more causalities.

The 500-man Haitian unit, Chasseurs-Volontaires de Saint-Domingue, was the largest unit of soldiers of African descent to fight in this war. The fact that their number was made up of freedmen who volunteered for this expedition is startling to most people and surprising to many historians. Twenty-five of their members have their names recorded as wounded or killed during the campaign. Over sixty would be captured in the fall of Charleston eight months later. Captured Haitian freedmen did not face the same consequences as others who were prisoners. The British Navy seized three transports carrying Chasseurs; these soldiers were made prizes of war and sold into slavery. The known prospect of being enslaved, a consequence other nationalities did not face, did not deter their loyalty to the cause. They served with recognition and honor.

Many of the Haitian soldiers later fought to win their country's own war of independence, crediting their military experience in Savannah as helpful. Influenced by both the events of the American Revolution and the rhetoric of the French Revolution, the people of Haiti began a struggle for self-government and liberty. Haiti would become the first nation in the Western Hemisphere to form a government led by people of African descent. This country was also the first nation to renounce slavery. (Their time spent in America with hopes of liberty for all had to make them long for a similar revolution in their own country.)

The Haitian Monument is the only one dedicated to Haitians in the United States and was a joint effort between the city of Savannah and the National Haitian Society. One of the Haitians who helped bring the monument into existence was Daniel Fils-Aime, chairman of the Miami-based Haitian American Historical Society, who said, "This is a testimony to tell people we Haitians didn't come from the boat. We were here in 1779 to help America win independence. That recognition is overdue."[89]

James Mastin was the sculptor. His artist statement is:

My goal as an artist is to communicate my sense of awe and wonder in the contemplation of the infinite human potential for creative expression, the unending attempt to balance the thirst for change against the fear of change.[90]

Mastin works in several different mediums, including oil painting and bas relief. He has several monuments to his credit: the Landing in Green Turtle Cay, Abaco, Bahamas; the Wreckers in Key West, Florida; Toussaint Loveture in Port au Prince, Haiti; and the bust of Loveture at his tomb in France. The latter two probably influenced his choice for this monument.

Originally, they did not have enough money to pay Mastin in full for the monument, so it was unveiled with only four of the soldiers. At the second unveiling, it caused a stir in the Haitian community. When the other two soldiers were revealed, the faces were familiar. The faces were a donor\politician and a Miami Haitian, who had been influential in the monument's creation. The first was Fils-Aime, a chairman of the Haitian-American Historical Society who had worked for more than nine years to raise money for the monument. The second was Rudolph Moise a Miami doctor and actor who had donated $120,000 toward its completion. Instantly, political rivals pointed out that Daniel Fils-Aime and Rudolph Moise played no part in the historic Savannah battle to preserve freedom and democracy. One critic, Phillip Brutus, said, "We think they are corrupting history. Everything in Haiti has been destroyed. The one thing Haitians can cling to and take pride in is that they are the first black republic of the world and that Haitian soldiers were instrumental in fighting for American independence. Haitians hold this very dear to their hearts. They take it very seriously, and when someone tampers with this, it unleashes all sorts of anger and anguish."[91]

Mastin, in an interview with *The Miami Herald*, said he picked Moise and Fils-Aime for their distinctive facial features, but was under no obligation to do so. Their rivals felt a coup of the monument had occurred. But Geoffrey Taylor, chairman of the department of art history at the Savannah College of Art and Design stated, "No one should be surprised an artist would look to living faces for his work." Artists "from the year zero to the present day" also have had to re-create and sometimes enhance details when depicting historic events.[92]

As for the question of patronage, that, too, would not be unusual, Taylor said. Works from the Italian Renaissance are replete with examples, especially those commissioned by the Vatican. Raphael often used Pope Leo X, his benefactor, to portray Pope Leo III and IV in paintings, Taylor noted. "Artists have been doing that for at least 1,000 years," he said. "It's a way of recognizing the beneficence of a patron in the guise of someone who you have no idea what they looked like."[93]

In a formal statement Mastin wrote:

I chose each of my models to best communicate the statement and feelings I hoped to convey with each of the six figures in the monument, and I selected based upon their size, posture, and facial characteristics. Daniel Fils-aime is exactly the look I wanted, and I decided over three years ago that I would use Mr. Fils-aime, although I sculpted a younger and slimmer version of him. All six of the figures I sculpted were based on one or more of the Haitian friends I have made through the various activities of the Haitian American Historical Society. In the case of Dr. Moise, I learned after I had chosen him as a model, that he would be contributing to HAHS efforts to put together a world-class monument in Savannah. If those complaining knew the identities of the other models for Les Chasseurs Volontaires, would they want them replaced as well? Though my choices were freely made, why not honor those who have worked so hard on behalf of the Haitian community?[94]

In the end, the "scandal" was probably much ado about nothing. There is not a thing that could and should take away from the helping hands and heroic deeds of these freedmen. Only a few people could know who these people were; to the majority of people who see the monument, they would not recognize them. (It is to the United States' shame that, years later, when the Haitians fought for *their* freedom, the Americans were not there to help them. But unlike America, whose independence was fought with international aid, the brave Haitians were alone in their independence fight.) Instead of assisting them, the US government feared that a successful slave revolt in Haiti would inspire a similar revolt in the United States. The US government thus used its influence in Haiti to promote repressive regimes after their war. Maybe this monument can act as a small thank you and a renewed partnership.

Flame of Freedom: We Hold These Truths to Be Self-evident

In front of the Chatham County Courthouse, an eternal flame stands. It is called the Flame of Freedom and was placed there by the local American Legion to celebrate its founding and fifty-year anniversary, in honor of all the veterans who have fought for our freedom.

Eternal flames can be seen all over the world. They can be found in use as far back as the Persians in 400 BCE. Used to promote cultural and religious concerns, in modern times, the flames are also erected to remind us of those who have sacrificed for our country

The Flame of Freedom.

and those who have lived truths that we promise to be ever vigilant to maintain. Here, in the United States, they can be found at the gravesites honoring President John F. Kennedy and Civil Rights Leader Martin Luther King Jr.

It seems appropriate to place an eternal flame in front of the courthouse. It serves as a reminder that the veterans of our nation give their lives to preserve equality under the law for all, the right to trial by a jury of our peers, the writ of habeas corpus, freedom of speech, and many other rights we have asked our judicial system to watch over. But it also reminds us we have all pledged as a nation to work to keep these rights self-evident.

The Flame of Freedom in front of the Chatham County Courthouse.

OTHER HISTORIC DISTRICT MONUMENTS

German Memorial: We Are Proud Americans

There were two major waves of Germanic immigrants to Savannah. The first wave was because of religious and economic causes in the early days of the colony. We have talked elsewhere of the Salzburgers, Moravians, and German Jews. These, and other Germans, would grow to approximately 1,000 German-speaking settlers. They were mostly from central and south Germany, Austria, and Switzerland.

The second migration was political and economic, occurring during the mid-nineteenth century, and it brought around 4,000 more Germans to Savannah. The Revolts of 1848 in Europe, as the peasantry rose up against the royalty causing major upheavals, was the impetus for the second migration to Savannah. These Germans spoke with a regional dialect and were found primarily in Northern Germany. Savannah's German-born population rapidly expanded and peaked in 1854. Among the newcomers were enterprising merchants and businessmen. Many were green grocers, tavern keepers, bakers, butchers, and cabinet makers. German traditions in food, drink, music, and entertainment blended with local traditions. The new arrival of Germanic people led to the founding of various community organizations.

In 1853, the Germania Fire Company was formed. This was one of several volunteer fire companies that were assigned specific wards of the city to protect. The Germania Fire Company oversaw Franklin and Ward Squares. They purchased the city's first steam-

Walkway to the German Memorial Fountain.

powered fire engine and, in the 1870s, built a magnificent fire house on West Congress Street.

The German Friendly Society of Savannah was organized on July 26, 1837, for the relief of indigent members, their widows and orphans, and to promote social and friendly harmony among the German community of Savannah. The motto of the Society still thriving today is "In essentials unity in non-essentials liberty, in all things charity."[95]

The influence and prominence of the Germans could be seen in their tall Germania bank building on the prestigious corner of Broughton and Bull streets, a newspaper in German, the

A picture of Oglethorpe Square with German Memorial Historical marker and fountain in the center.

German Memorial Fountain.

rise of several Lutheran congregations and church buildings, especially the historic Evangelical Lutheran Church of the Ascension, and the prominent German country club.

The influence of Germans in the building of the Central of Georgia Railroad was crucial. Nicholas Cruger was the engineer who laid out the route of the line to Macon. Augustus Schwaab became chief engineer and designed Kiah Hall (Gray Building), the North Viaduct on West Boundary Street, the Savannah Visitors Center, as well as the City Market. The founding of the Telfair Museum of Art attracted three Germans of significant influence to Savannah: Carl Brandt became its first director. Architect Detleif Lineau, born in Schleswig-Holstein, built the museum rotunda and additions. He

would also design Hodgson Hall for the Georgia Historical Society and devise modifications to the Wayne-Gordon House. Brandt commissioned statuary of great masters to grace the Telfair Museum's entrance. Wurtemburger John Walz was sent to install them. He eventually set up shop in Savannah and his statuary and bas reliefs are found on the US Courthouse, Chatham Academy's Oglethorpe Avenue façade, the Scottish Rite Lodge, and Little Gracie at Bonaventure Cemetery. Thomas Purse, a charter member of the Evangelical Lutheran Church of the Ascension, became mayor in 1861.[96]

Yet, the proud Germans would face challenges during the two great wars in which the United States participated against the German Empire. Although the Savannah German community would join with their fellow Americans in this fight against the Germans, they would become less visible because of the times. For example, the German Friendly Society would change their name to The Lexington Society on June 23, 1918. The Society operated under this name until February 16, 1929. On January 13, 1942, the name was once again changed to The Friendly Society of Savannah, Inc. The present name, The German Friendly Society of Savannah, Inc., was voted into existence on December 10, 1965.[97]

In 1962, a renewal of pride began to take place and the German Savannahians began a process of reclaiming their heritage in the forming of the German Heritage Society. This resurgence would continue in 1983, when the Savannah

A close-up of the frogs on the German Memorial Fountain.

Toomer Monument.

Toomer Monument.

Waterfront Association organized an annual Oktoberfest celebration. Furthermore, at the 250th anniversary of Savannah's founding, in 1989, when the Scots and Jews were erecting their celebratory monuments, the German-descended community dedicated the German Memorial Fountain here in Orleans Square. It is with this memorial they reclaimed their proud place in Savannah and its history.

Toomer Monument:
Brother Can You Spare a Dime?

Martin Luther King Jr. Boulevard was once called West Broad Street. West Broad Street was where the black community conducted business, shopped, and listened to music before integration. King Oliver, a jazz legend and mentor of Louis Armstrong, lived his final years here. The black community found opportunity with local black-owned businesses in this location. It was Savannah's "Harlem."

Louis B. Toomer saw an opportunity to help build the community and founded Carver State Bank in 1927. This bank was the first locally owned bank in Savannah and was also the fourth oldest commercial bank in the United States owned by African-Americans. Toomer's business acumen led the bank through the Great Depression and helped him start successful insurance and real estate companies.

But Toomer was more than a businessman. Bob James, current president of Carver State Bank, said, "Toomer believed that it was important for African-American business leaders to be involved in civic affairs and this commitment to community service and civic participation has continued as a guiding principal for the organization over the years."[98] Because of his national business reputation and his involvement in Republican politics, he was appointed Registrar of the Treasury by President Dwight D. Eisenhower and served from 1953 to 1956.

One of the two Carver Banks still stands on West Broad Street, but the street is not the economic and cultural hub of the black community anymore. Urban renewal decided it was best to build highway I-16 in the middle of it and, with the advent of integration, many blacks started shopping in white businesses or were able to have their companies in other areas of town. These and other issues led to the slow demise of West Broad Street. Yet Toomer and other entrepreneurs of West Broad Street showed that if given a fair chance they, too, could succeed.

Semiquincentenary Fountain: We Have Been Around for Quite Some Time

In 1983, it was the 250th year of the founding of Savannah, and Savannahians wanted to celebrate their proud heritage. Part of the events to herald the anniversary was the erection of several monuments built by the various ethnic groups who had made Savannah the thriving city it was. The Scots, Germans, Irish, and Jewish communities all commemorated the anniversary with various monuments. Not since the boom of the nineteenth century had so many been erected. These works, while smaller, without prominent artists, and not always found in the squares of Bull Street as in the nineteenth century, were nonetheless built with as much pride as the others.

The Semiquincentenary Fountain was designed as a testimony to the ongo-

Picture of the cranes on the Semiquincentenary Fountain.

ing spirit and heritage that Savannahians, as a whole, shared with their ancestors of 250 years earlier. The Colonial Dames of America donated this three-tiered, Verde antique, cast-iron fountain to the city. It sits in Lafayette Square in the shadow of the huge Gothic St. John's Cathedral. Also on the Square is the childhood home of one of Savannah's most prominent citizens: author Flannery O'Connor. She is noted for her short stories about Southerners, as well as her unique personality.

Lafayette Square with the Semiquincentenary Fountain in the center.

Semiquincentenary Fountain.

The Fountain is surrounded by two structures that represent much of the greatness attributed to Savannah: architecture, arts, and in O'Connor, a truly Southern quirkiness.

Armillary:
Where in the World Are We?

There was a proposal to cut service roads through some of the squares to enable emergency vehicles and buses to travel more easily. Fire engines had grown to the point that they no longer could maneuver around the squares because the turns were not wide enough. Clermont Huger Lee, a native Savannahian and the first female professional landscape architect to open a private practice in the city, stepped in. She had attended Smith College, where she majored in landscape architecture. After completing her undergraduate degree, she attended the Graduate School of Architecture and Landscape Architecture, where she obtained her master's in landscape architecture, also from Smith College. She became one of the few women members of the American Society of Landscape Architects and a founder of the Georgia Landscape Association, as well as the first woman landscape architect in Georgia.

In the early 1950s, Lee began her involvement in historic landscapes. Her designs are found throughout Savannah: in the gardens of the Owens-Thomas House on Oglethorpe Square, the birthplace of Girl Scout founder Juliette Gordon Low, the Andrew Low House, and the Green-Meldrim mansion. She also was the landscape designer of four squares in Savannah: Madison, Troup,

Armillary sphere that sits in the center of Troup Square.

Warren, and Washington.[99] Her solution to prevent the paving of roads through the middle of the squares was to round the corners of the squares and the streets surrounding them allowing emergency vehicles and buses to maneuver around the squares and preserve them from the onslaught of tarred roads.

Troup Square was one of four that she and philanthropist Mills Lane Jr. worked on together. Working in the mid-twentieth century, Lee was an expert in recreating historic landscapes. In this square and the others her meticulously studied work of gardens in England and the antebellum period can be seen.

She chose as the centerpiece of Troup Square to be an armillary. Some sources credit Greek philosopher Anaximander of Miletus with inventing the armillary sphere, while others credit Greek astronomer Hipparchus, and some credit the Chinese, whose armillaries first

Notice the curved corner.

Notice the golden zodiac sign and sphere sitting on the backs of turtles.

appeared during the Han Dynasty. One early Chinese armillary can be traced to Zhang Heng, an astronomer in the Eastern Han Dynasty. An armillary is a model of the stars and planets in the sky centered on Earth (after Copernicus, the armillary was modeled to revolve around the sun); the spheres represent lines of celestial longitude and latitude and other astronomically important features to locate various objects in the sky.

This armillary was made by a family firm, Kenneth Lynch and Sons, that began in Connemara, Ireland, some 300 years ago. The firm was involved with many famous projects, including the 1939 New York World's Fair, as well as endeavors by

metalworker Samuel Yellin and sculptor Paul Manship.[100] The armillary was ordered from the firm's catalogue.

The beauty that you see in this square combines the work and efforts of native Savannahians who loved and cared for their hometown.

Myers Drinking Fountain: I Love This City

Savannah's first Jewish mayor was also one of Savannah's greatest mayors. Herman Myers was mayor from 1895 to 1907, except for a two-year interval. He died on March 24, 1909, but during his terms as mayor, City Hall and the Union Railroad Station were erected. The City Hall, with its gold dome and Beaux Arts style by architect Hyman Witcover, was considered the best city hall south of Richmond. Witcover was an important Savannah architect. He was the architect for such buildings as the current Savannah College of Art and Design Student Center, which was originally the B'inai B'rith Synagogue, the Scottish Rite Temple, Savannah's main library, and the Effingham County Courthouse.

The Union Station was the proud entry point of people to Savannah until the 1950s, when it was razed to make room for Interstate 16. Upon Meyers' death, it is recalled of his funeral, "thousands of persons from every walk in life and all ages went to the City Hall to get a last look at the man who in life did so much for Savannah."[101]

The Myers Drinking Fountain was donated by him in 1888 for Forsyth Park. The fountain stood nine feet tall and was said, "to be dispensing its sparkling

Blacksmith Ivan Bailey placed his trademark sunflowers on the side.

nectar to the thousands that throng that delightful spot."[102] At the top was a classically draped female figure holding a dove—this top was lost while it was in storage. The fountain was removed from Forsyth Park, no one knows today why, and put in storage for many years. Later it was "discovered" the bottom of the fountain was missing.

The Myers Drinking Fountain. This Fountain once stood in Forsyth Park for visitors to have a drink. It was restored by sculptor Ivan Bailey and the remaining parts made into a fountain for dogs.

It was decided at this time to be placed in Troup Square. Ivan Bailey, a blacksmith and the sculptor of the Olympic Torch Monument, was hired to reconfigure this one. Because the bottom was missing it was turned into a fountain not only for humans, but the bottom has a place for canines to drink too. Bailey also put his signature sunflowers on the sides.

The monument is small, but touches as many people as the much larger projects of City Hall and Union Station, and I know it pleases more dogs.

Cisterns Marker:
Enough Water to Quench a Thirst

Before there was running water, plumbing, and fire hydrants, there were cisterns. It appears that one of the first projects after the laying out of the squares was to dig cisterns to supply water for cooking, cleaning, and drinking. They were the inner city equivalent of wells. They may be filled with rainwater or groundwater. The cistern in Wright Square was "rediscovered" in 2012. Workers came upon an unidentified manhole cover under a pad of concrete below a bench. It was larger and heavier than most. Upon exploration, they found a round cistern about 13.5 feet high and fourteen feet in diameter, capable of holding 16,000 gallons of water. It appeared in perfect shape. The cistern was not on any of the city maps available, so the workers mapped it and sealed the manhole cover.[103]

We know that cisterns exist at least in Madison, Wright, Washington, and Crawford Squares, as well as some others. Because of the location of the Fire Department on Washington Square, its cistern, and that of its sister square Crawford, was used primarily for firefighting. Crawford Square would have been laid out twenty-one years after the Great Savannah Fire of 1820, in 1841. The obvious need for water—and plenty of it—had been proven by the Great Fire.

The Crawford Square Cistern is open, so that you can see the outside of its finely made exterior. It was the design and work of two of Savannah's most accomplished men: architect William Clusky and master builder Amos Scudder. Clusky designed one of Savannah's finest homes, the Sorrel Weed House, and the governor's mansion in Milledgeville. Scudder

oversaw the construction of the original Independent Presbyterian Church, designed several homes in the Historic District, and was responsible for the building of Savannah's first canal system, which he later used for himself when he bought the canal system from the city.

This particular cistern was nine feet, two inches to thirteen feet, five inches and was built in the 1830s and

The marker about the cisterns in front of the gazebo in Crawford Square.

'40s. We often forget the work and the people who created the remarkable infrastructure systems of our cities. But here we see the skill and craftsmanship of two of Savannah's finest builders of their day. The combination of the noted designer and builder is a reminder of the importance put on the infrastructure of the city.

Uncovered cistern in Crawford Square.

Crawford Square Recreation: Where Everyone Knows Your Name

The story of Crawford Square is the story of race in Savannah. The square is named after the distinguished Georgian William Crawford, who served as President James Madison's Minister to France and Secretary of War from 1815 to 1816. He also served as Secretary of Treasury from 1816 to 1825, during Madison's and Monroe's presidencies. Another claim to fame for this square is that Lady Chablis of the *Midnight in the Garden of Good and Evil* book\movie fame lived here.

The square was the only one that African-Americans were allowed to use during the Jim Crow era of laws and cultural practices to enforce segregation. Coincidently or not, it is also one of the smallest squares in Savannah, yet Crawford Ward is the largest ward in Savannah. It is also the only square that has recreational use and there is a basketball court and playground equipment that other squares do not have. Because the squares are one of the main attractions of Savannah's tourism, from time to time an argument comes, primarily from white officials and developers: the square should be made to conform to the rest of the Squares. Crawford Square should be more like a garden in its usage and appearance, they say. The black community resists this change because of the part this square has played in their community's history. In fact, there is a book written about the Square by a former resident called *Remembering Crawford Square*.

This monument, which talks about recreation in the Square, emphasizes the role the square played in the lives of Savannah's black community. In 1946, when the city held its first citywide

Plaque honoring recreation in Crawford Square. Notice the basketball goal won in a citywide basketball tournament by the Crawford Square team.

basketball tournament, the Crawford Square young men won the tournament and the right to have a basketball court installed in their namesake square. The court was constructed in 1947 and brought a great sense of pride in the Ward, whose story is still told and here memorialized.

Today, the city holds a high school basketball tournament during December called the Savannah Holiday Tournament. One of the two boys' divisions in the Tournament is called Crawford Square.

The Crawford Square and Ward are facing racial and economic gentrification today. Yet, if one listens carefully, one can hear the joy of this Ward in 1947 as a "small" victory held the promise of a better day ahead for their children and grandchildren in a time when Jim Crow and the KKK flourished. The small victory in 1947 will always remain as part of the local lore of another time if we care to cherish all the stories of our city.

Second African Baptist Church: Together We Cannot Be Defeated

Savannah's African-American citizens have always been leaders in the national community for advancing the rights of blacks. The First African Baptist Church was built by the hands of free blacks and slaves; it is the first black church in America. They also built their church with an underground tunnel that led to the Savannah River. The church itself was built four feet off the ground with openings in the basement floor in a geometrical pattern to provide breathing holes for the slaves who were hidden beneath. They were a part of the Underground Railroad. First African Baptist's sixth pastor was Reverend Emmanuel King Love; he was influential in the establishment of three historically black universities: Savannah State University, formerly known as Georgia State Industrial College for Colored Youth; Morehouse College in Atlanta; and Paine College in Augusta, Georgia.[104]

In 1942, before the modern Civil Rights Movement began, under the leadership of First African Baptist Church's minister Reverend Ralph Mark Gilbert, the Savannah National Association for the Advancement of Colored People branch was reorganized. Shortly thereafter, Gilbert convened the first state conference of the NAACP. He was elected as president and, during his eight years of leadership of the state NAACP, more than forty branches were organized in Georgia by 1950. Also through Gilbert's efforts the Savannah Police Department would have some of

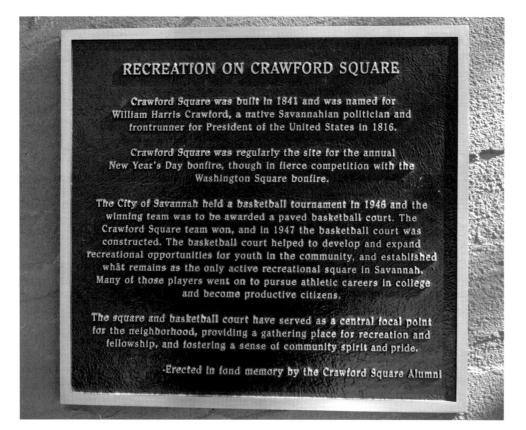

RECREATION ON CRAWFORD SQUARE

Crawford Square was built in 1841 and was named for William Harris Crawford, a native Savannahian politician and frontrunner for President of the United States in 1816.

Crawford Square was regularly the site for the annual New Year's Day bonfire, though in fierce competition with the Washington Square bonfire.

The City of Savannah held a basketball tournament in 1946 and the winning team was to be awarded a paved basketball court. The Crawford Square team won, and in 1947 the basketball court was constructed. The basketball court helped to develop and expand recreational opportunities for youth in the community, and established what remains as the only active recreational square in Savannah. Many of those players went on to pursue athletic careers in college and become productive citizens.

The square and basketball court have served as a central focal point for the neighborhood, providing a gathering place for recreation and fellowship, and fostering a sense of community spirit and pride.

-Erected in fond memory by the Crawford Square Alumni

Recreation in Crawford Square plaque.

House, which was the headquarters of General Sherman during the Civil War. In the Green-Meldrim meeting they were asked what "did they need" most, in lieu of liberation; the black leadership said land. A few days later, it was from the steps of the old wooden Second African Baptist Church that General Sherman read the Emancipation Proclamation to Savannah's citizens gathered in Greene Square, and promised the 1,000 newly freed slaves "40 acres and a mule" in Field Order Number Fifteen.

Marker with Second African Baptist Church in background.

the first black police officers in the South in 1947.[105] Today, the local Civil Rights Museum is named after Gilbert.

Despite resistance from some local whites, First African Baptist Church's membership grew to over 2,000 in the late eighteenth century. Because of this phenomenal growth, they felt a need to develop another congregation. It should come as no surprise that the church they would commission would also be tied to two of the most significant events in American history.

The Second African Baptist Church dates back to 1802. The present church was built in 1925 after fire destroyed the first church. The church was able to save the original pulpit, prayer benches, and choir chairs. In 1864, the pastor and church played host to Secretary of War Edwin M. Stanton and General William T. Sherman. Leaders of the black community had previously met with them at the historic Green-Meldrim

The marker at the church was the site of the forty acres and a mule order, as well as a practice run of Martin Luther King Jr.'s "I Have a Dream" speech.

Prominent members of Second African Baptist Church and the black community in Savannah were the DeVeaux family. At a time when it was illegal, Jane DeVeaux established a secret school to teach African-Americans to read and write; the school would meet for thirty years in secret, only ending with the close of the Civil War. *The Colored Tribune* newspaper was founded in 1875 by Colonel John DeVeaux. In 1878, he was forced to close the paper because white printers in the city refused to print it, but he reopened the publication, known today as the *Savannah Tribune*, in 1886. The weekly newspaper is still in existence today.

In 1963, Martin Luther King Jr. came to a Sunday service and was asked to speak from the pulpit. He recited the last lines of what later would become his famous "I Have a Dream" speech.

Savannah's black community has offered so much to the nation and has made Savannah what it is today. Despite the once horrendous conditions Savannah's black community lived under, they have risen and continue to share their dreams and visions for Savannah.

Washington Firehouse Marker: Thanks for the Memories

Savannah's first large fire was in 1796, when much of the commercial district was burned; the fire destroyed 226 buildings. In 1820, what has been called the Great Savannah Fire burned almost 500 structures, with damages of about $4 million.[106] The first organized fire department was established five years later, on March 11, 1825, when the City Council appointed twenty persons to form the Savannah Fire Company. In the early days, there were no salaries paid and the City Council filled all vacancies. "Free men of color, free Negroes, and hired slaves" performed firefighting duties, took part in a schedule of monthly drills, and kept up apparatus maintenance. In that day, the mayor and aldermen were required to attend fires! (Talk about your nice constituent services.)

The Savannah Fire Company was divided up, and foremen were assigned to manage the black firemen of the different engines; the foremen were called "Masters of Engines." Slave owners were expected to provide slave assistance and Masters of Engines were authorized to administer "prompt and immediate correction" whenever a slave "disobeyed or otherwise offended." At first, the firefighters were paid a certain amount for being the first to respond to the fire and the amount would decrease according to the order in which one responded. Each slave fireman was provided with a badge, which entitled him to the "immunities and privileges of a fireman."[107]

Eventually, as firefighters were paid and achieved prominence in the community, the ranks of the firefighters were filled with whites only. White "toughs" would run off the black firefighters and claim the honor of extinguishing fires for themselves. By 1860, the Savannah Fire Company consisted of fourteen fire companies. Four independent white companies had been formed and ten "colored"

Washington Fire Company marker.

companies, which were from the original Savannah Fire Company. It would not be until May 1, 1963, that the fire department would be integrated, although extra living and sleeping quarters were put in the back to separate them from the white firefighters. The Savannah Fire Company, in 1911, became the first fully-mechanized fire department in the US.

Through the years, the stations and the firefighters played an important part in their communities. This marker is dedicated to two of Savannah's fire companies. The First Fire Station was No. 1, built at 522 East Broughton Street in 1878 and remaining there until 1959. The cornerstone of that station is in the base of this marker. The predecessor of that station was Washington Fire Company No. 9. The Washington Fire Company was located on Washington Square and served and protected the surrounding area for twenty-four years. These two stations not only acted as establishments for fighting fires, but they also assumed the atmosphere of a community center. Retired Captain Arthur Watson served at No. 1 for the last eleven years it was in operation. "I think that No. 1 on Broughton Street was probably the greatest thing that ever happened to this neighborhood," he said, "because everything that happened here was centered around No. 1. All your people came and went. They brought their problems and we tried to solve them; we tried to help them every way we could. That went on when I was a child, and it went on when I was a fireman."[108]

One of the men influenced by these firefighters, Ted Haviland, grew up in the neighborhood and spent many an hour at No. 1 hanging around firemen like Watson. Haviland wanted to make sure both fire stations were remembered. So, he spent a long time petitioning the Metropolitan Planning Commission and the city of Savannah for permission to build a small monument in Washington Square: the monument you now see. Many years have passed since the freed blacks and slaves worked to stop fires, but the same bravery of the firefighters is viewed each time they respond to a call.

Bell at International Seamen's House: Home Sweet Home

The Savannah Port Society was formed by the Georgia Legislature in 1843. Its purpose was to promote the welfare of "seaman frequenting the Port of Savannah." The first meeting was held at the Independent Presbyterian Church on November 21, 1843. This was the beginning of a ministry that has lasted well over 150 years. Through those many years, the Society has aided sailors from all over the world with their spiritual and physical needs.

In 1943, the Society formed the International Seaman's House to provide hospitality services to sailors far from home. Today, it offers transportation services for shopping and other needs; telephone services, including inexpensive phone cards and placement of cell phones on board vessels; Internet access; game tables; donated clothes, refreshments, literature/media resources, and religious services—all at no cost to the seafarers.

The bell in honor of the Seaman's House chaplain.

A close-up of the bell at the International Seaman's House.

The House served over 7,000 seamen from fifty-eight countries that came to Savannah in 2012.[109]

This tradition of hospitality to sailors has been carried on by chaplains and volunteers from the community. The bell honors one of the most beloved chaplains, Reverend Dale Umbreit, who served in that capacity for thirteen years. Alongside the bell are cornerstones of other buildings of the Savannah Port Society and a plaque to one of the maritime community's leaders, John Hohenstein Jr., partner in Hohenstein Shipping Company.

Nearly 3,000 vessels dock in Savannah each year loading or unloading commodities from around the world. The sailors, many knowing no English and dependent on the kindness of strangers, are sometimes greeted by the volunteers

OTHER HISTORIC DISTRICT MONUMENTS

The porch at the International Seaman's House.

and chaplains who offer a hand of friendship. The International Seamen's House is known by commercial seamen as their "Home away from home."

Wormsloe Fountain:
Getting Back to Our Roots

In Columbia Square we see two important events that lay the foundation of Savannah's history. Columbia refers to the female personification of the United States. Columbia Square was constructed in 1799. The Fountain within it is sometimes called the "rustic fountain" because of the vines, leaves, flowers and other nature motifs found on it. The Fountain itself once sat on the Wormsloe Plantation, the home of one of the original settlers of Georgia, Noble Jones. It was moved to Columbia Square, in 1970, in honor of two of

Wormsloe Fountain in the middle of Columbia Square.

The fountain is sometimes referred to as the "Rustic Fountain" because of the tree and plants on the base.

Close-up of "Rustic Fountain."

Noble Jones's descendants: Augusta and Wimberly Derenne. This monument is a piece of history from the Jones's estate from the colonial period and is given in honor of two of his descendants who, in modern times, continued to care and preserve Savannah. The connection ranges from the origins of Georgia to modern Savannah.

But there is an even more significant reason why the Square was being revitalized and the fountain placed there. The famed Davenport House sits on Columbia Square. This historic home, made by master shipbuilder Isaiah Davenport, became the site of the struggle that would establish Savannah's Historic Foundation. In 1955, the Davenport House was facing the wrecking ball, just as other Savannah historic sites, such as the old Desoto Hotel and the old City Market had already experienced. The successful effort to save the Davenport House became the building ground for the Historic Savannah Foundation, an organization that has saved and preserved over 350 homes. Today, the Foundation is the leader in the preservationist movement in Savannah. The Davenport House was the first headquarters of the Historic Savannah Foundation.

The Fountain is a reminder of the colonial days, but also was brought to this place to celebrate the new preservationist movement in Savannah. Here, in its rustic style, the city of Savannah is confronted with its past and its future and displays how the two will always be linked.

Police Officers' Monument: To Protect and To Serve

Memory is a key ingredient to religious life. Jews are to remember the Sabbath and, at Passover, they are to remember when God delivered them out of Egypt. Asian religions place a high value in remembering their ancestors. It is also a large part of what could be called our civil religion. We do not forget the great deeds of our presidents, prophets, or popular citizens.

We choose as a society to remember our soldiers who have died in battle. And here, with this monument, we choose to hold up the lives of those police officers who died in service to their communities.

The trial of the murder of Patrolman Harry H. Akins was in court in 1963. Akins, who was only twenty-five years old, was shot and killed investigating a burglary. The owner of the service station he was searching shot through the door and mortally wounded him. Nell Fountain, president of the Police Officers' Wives Association, looked at the young wife of slain Patrolman Akins and pledged that a memorial would be made for officers killed in the line of duty.[110]

The site for the monument was dedicated June 12, 1964. The base was designed and fabricated by Graham C. Legget, owner of Leggett Marble and Granite Company of Savannah, and was dedicated without the policeman figure on September 21, 1964. The model for the police officer was carved out of wood by G.W. Woods, a local woodcarver, in 1965. Woods used a city patrolman named R.I. Ketterman as his model.

Police Officers' Monument.

ABOVE AND BEYOND
"LEST WE FORGET"

SAVANNAH POLICE OFFICERS

SAMUEL BRYSON	1868
ROBERT E. READ	1868
JOHN DAN SULLIVAN	1869
HABERSHAM W. HARVEY	1881
PATRICK McMURRAY	1888
J. C. NEVE	1894
WALTER H. MARLOWE	1921
PHILLIP E. STEEVES	1922
WILLIAM F. HODGES	1924
ALBERT LAMB	1926
WILLIAM C. ELLZEY	1926
O. RAYMOND HUGHES	1928
SAMUEL WEBB	1929
HERBERT V. FITZGERALD	1929
ROBERT B. RAYPER	1932
JAMES E. ROUGHEN	1934
JOHN J. O'REILLY	1939
EARL W. EUBANKS	1941
JAMES WALTER TODD	1949
H DAN ROLISON	1960
JIMMY LEE BLA	1966
FRANK W. MOBLE	1968
ROBERT DAVID WATFORD	1969
JAMES W. ARCHBAN	1970

Base of the Police Officers' Monument listing the names of the officers killed on duty.

Engraved on the granite below the patrolman are fifty-one names. They begin with the names Patrolman Samuel Bryson and Patrolman Robert Read, who were shot and killed while attempting to restore order during a race riot that broke out during the 1868 presidential election. The riot was started by citizens opposing candidate Ulysses S. Grant. (The officers probably did not support either candidate, but it was their job and calling to keep order.)

Every year in mid-May, on Police Officers' Memorial Day, a service is held at the monument by the historic Savannah police barracks (the oldest continuously used barracks in the United States). Families, officers, dignitaries, and others gather and a red rose is placed in front of the monument in honor of each of the officers. "Taps" is played. Names are called. Officers are remembered. We as a city fulfill our pledge to these and all officers: if you die in the line of duty, we will remember you and thank you for giving your life to protect and serve us.

Button Gwinnett Monument: Can't a Fellow Have a Moment's Peace?

The most interesting bone story in Savannah is not that of Nathanael Greene or Casimir Pulaski, but the story of Button Gwinnett. Button Gwinnett was Savannah's only signer of the Declaration of Independence—and also the signer we know the least about. He died before the signers would become revered as they are now. His life was cut short by a duel, making him the first signer to die. The short life and the few

Button Gwinnett Monument in Colonial Cemetery in downtown Savannah.

OTHER HISTORIC DISTRICT MONUMENTS

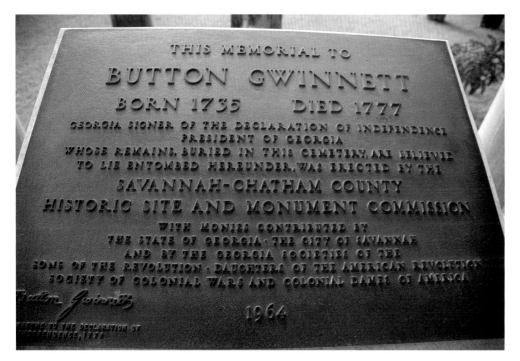

Plaque commemorating Button Gwinnett.

at the estate of Governor Wright near the small town of Thunderbolt outside of Savannah. Both men fired almost simultaneously and both were struck. McIntosh survived, but Gwinnett died three days later, when his shattered leg bone turned gangrenous. McIntosh was later accused of murder, but was exonerated in an official inquiry.[111]

Many years later, in 1957, retired school principal Authur Funk was at the National Portrait Gallery gazing at a painting of the signers of the Declaration of Independence. Being a Savannahian, he noticed the absence of Button Gwinnett. When Funk asked the curator why this was, the curator stated that there was not much information about Gwinnett and especially how he looked. This sparked an interest in Funk that would lead him in search of the historical Button Gwinnett and to the development of a monument to Gwinnett.

One of the first things Funk decided to do was to locate where Gwinnett was buried. It turned out no one really knew. In a city that prided itself on preserving its history, they had no idea where its signer of the Declaration of Independence was buried. Funk eventually came across some documents that led his search to the historic Colonial Cemetery in downtown Savannah. After much exploration, Funk found where he believed Gwinnett was buried and, upon digging, found what he believed were the remains of Gwinnett. The bones he found were to create quite a stir.

He immediately sent the bones to an expert affiliated with the Smithsonian Institute. The Smithsonian expert said

copies of his signature is why it is the most valuable of all of the signers.

In his fleeting moment on this earth he was able to accomplish a lot. He wrote the draft of Georgia's first state constitution, was a prosperous planter, became speaker of the general assembly in Georgia, and the governor of Georgia. The infamous duel was with his chief political rival Lachlan McIntosh.

While in Congress, Gwinnett was in line with McIntosh to be the Brigadier General of the Georgia Continental Brigade, which was being organized. Gwinnett was passed over and McIntosh was made the general. While in office, Gwinnett organized an invasion of the British-held east Florida to ensure that

the Spanish did not hold any ideas of invasion or encroachment, while the colony was at war with Britain. Gwinnett wanted to lead these troops himself, but as a busy governor it was not possible. Bypassing rival McIntosh, Gwinnett appointed another officer to lead the military effort. The invasion was a disaster. This likely caused Gwinnett to lose the election for governor in 1777. During Gwinnett's run for office, McIntosh openly blamed Gwinnett for the failed campaign. Gwinnett, who was cleared of wrongdoing in a formal inquiry, felt that McIntosh's public criticism questioned his honor. He formally challenged McIntosh to a duel. The two met on May 16, 1777, these were not the bones of Gwinnett. But some of the expert's findings were based on false and misguided premises. Other experts would contradict the Smithsonian's expert. Eventually, to try to get clarification on the matter, the state of Georgia would create a commission to make the final official judgment of whether these bones were indeed Gwinnett's.

To add to the intrigue, the city of Augusta, Georgia, laid claim to the bones. Augusta had a signer's monument in their downtown that already had

Entrance to Colonial Cemetery.

Georgia's other two signers (Lyman Hall and George Walton) buried beneath it. Therefore, in a formal letter, Augusta's mayor and city council contended they had rights to the remains to Gwinnett's remains. The Savannah and Augusta papers were filled with editorials claiming the bones for their respective cities. This is how the great battle for Gwinnett's bones began.

Mayor Beckum of Augusta produced an old newspaper story of 1948 stating that Augusta had left a warm place for Gwinnett to be buried under their Signers' Monument. Savannah countered by quoting the 1895 contract, which transferred the title of Christ Church cemetery to the city. The contracts states that the hallowed ground shall forever be preserved as a "final resting place of the dead now buried therein." Removing Gwinnett's bones, Savannahians said, would therefore be illegal.[112] The battle pressed on but, in truth, no state official wanted to handle this hot potato.

During all of this, Funk ran for state representative from the Savannah area. He won and found himself in the governing body of Georgia. Although he said it was not the reason he had run for office, he put forth legislation for funding a monument in Savannah to honor the remains of Gwinnett. The state commission disputed the findings of the Smithsonian expert point by point in their report and declared that most likely they were the bones of Gwinnett. The Augusta mayor, upon hearing the decision and realizing the legislation was going to pass for the monument to be in

Savannah, replied with a pout, "If we do not know they are Gwinnett's bones, we do not want them anyway."

Indeed, the vote did pass the legislature. But not before Spencer Grayson, another Savannah delegate, declared jokingly, "I only voted for this measure to get Gwinnett's bones out of Senator Funk's living room."[113] Because the issue of the true proprietorship of the bones was in question and the fear of grave robbers, Funk had the remains in a sealed coffin in his house for the prior five and a half years. Legend says Funk replied, "Why sir, I am too much of a gentleman to leave such a prominent guest in the living room; he is in my guest room."

The monument was placed where Funk originally found Gwinnett's bones in Colonial Cemetery. An engraving of a copy of Gwinnett's signature sits on a plaque underneath the Roman style monument. Many tourists make rubbings of this signature. Funk also requested that the plaque also read: "Beneath this monument lies the remains of Savannah's signer of the Declaration of Independence, Button Gwinnett." He would have the last word about where the body of Gwinnett rest.

Today, years later tourists visit historic Colonial Cemetery and see the monument honoring Gwinnett. Few will realize that his remains had been lost, found, fought for, and legislated as being his. No, a tourist will simply think, nice monument, and believe Button Gwinnett has always been known and honored at this his gravesite.

Big Duke Fire Bell:
When He Speaks Everyone Listens

Savannah had a problem. There were plenty of small fire bells for various wards and firehouses, but no big bell that could be heard throughout the city. This is where "Big Duke," weighing in at 5,500 pounds, came to the rescue in 1872. It was big and it could be heard. It was named after Alderman and Fire Commissioner Marmaduke Hamilton, who was the chief instigator behind the purchase of the bell. Big Duke led a loud and proud life until 1890. That year the fire call was abolished because the volunteer fire department was replaced by full-time professional firefighters, who were always on hand at the fire house and did not need to be beckoned with the call of "Big Duke."

Normally, a bell such as this would have faced permanent retirement, but the public and firefighters had grown accustomed to Big Duke's sound and slowly transformed it from a bell for utility to a bell for memorial. In 1968, Big Duke was moved to its current location and, in 1985, it was declared a memorial to firefighters of all nations. An obelisk was placed here, in 1993, that reads in part: Where Firefighters Are Honored. Those That Live With Dignity Should Be Remembered With Honor.

The names of the firefighters who have died on the job are listed on the monument, including John Butler, the first firefighter who perished working in the Great Savannah Fire in 1865. Once a year, a memorial service is held for those firefighters who have given their lives. After the name of each firefighter

Big Duke in all its glory.

The Fire Department Memorial with the names of firefighters killed on duty.

is called, it is followed by the ringing of "Big Duke." For whom does the bell toll? It tolls for brave firefighters who we all should remember.

Moravian Monument:
A Faith as Old as Time Itself

The Moravians were one set of immigrants who came to America seeking religious freedom. They were organized in 1457 in Kunvald, 100 miles east of Prague. Jan Hus was burned at the stake by the Catholic Church for heresy. He anticipated the Protestant Reformation in the sixteenth century by his opinions about the Eucharist. In fact, during one of Martin Luther's heresy trials, he was accused of being a follower of Jan Hus. Luther vehemently denied this charge, only to study during a break in the trials who Hus was and wrote back to his accusers "We are all Hussites without knowing it."[114] His teachings had a strong influence on Czechoslovakia, where the Moravians had their start. Between 1420 and 1431, the Hussite followers defeated five consecutive attempts by the Vatican to put down the "uprising" of the followers of Hus.[115] History would label these struggles as the Hussite Wars. A century later, as many as ninety percent of inhabitants of the Czech lands were non-Catholic and followed the teachings of Hus and his successors.[116] The Moravians or Unitas Fratrum, Unity of Brethren, were part of the legacy of Hus.

The Moravians saw the new Georgia Colony as an opportunity to further their missionary outreach during the mid-eighteenth century to unite Christians and convert non-Christians. Their campaigns included efforts in Africa, the Caribbean, India, North America (including Greenland), Suriname, and much of Europe. Other Protestant groups were wary of the Moravians because of their ecumenism and their inclusion of women as preachers, as well as for their ability to hold religious offices.

Forty-one Moravians made their first pilgrimage to the new land of America in 1735. On their journey aboard ship, John Wesley, the founder of Methodism, would be greatly influenced by these courageous and pious people. They would be in Georgia for ten years living in a communal settlement in Savannah. They had hoped to join efforts with the Salzburgers, but because of

The Moravian Monument.

theological and church politics, as well as the Salzburgers' need for isolation and independence, the Moravians would stay in Ebenezer upriver of Savannah.

The Moravians' religious convictions would repeatedly come into conflict with their fellow colonists. The Moravians led efforts to convert Native Americans and slaves across the River in Purysburgh, South Carolina, but because of the struggle with Spain that began in 1739, their mission with the Native Americans was eventually ended. The conflict also increased the colonists' desire for everyone to bear arms. The Moravians were pacifists and refused to participate in the arming of the colony for battle with the Spaniards. This did not sit well with the other colonists. While the slaves resisted their evangelical efforts, the slave owners did not approve of attempts at bringing their "property" into the Christian faith.[117] If slaves became their Christian brothers and sisters, holding them in slavery would not be acceptable.

Meanwhile, the Salzburgers and famed evangelist George Whitefield (the new rector who had replaced Wesley) did not appreciate the Moravians' religious practices and were in constant disagreement with them. All of these factors, plus internal differences in the communal life of the Moravians, led to their departure from Savannah ten years after they had made their start here. Some Moravians returned to Europe, but most joined other Moravians in Bethlehem and Nazareth, Pennsylvania, to start very successful Moravian communities there.

In 1800, the Tennessee Wachovian Moravians sent missionaries to Georgia. They had missions to the Cherokees at Spring Place, in present-day Murray County (near the Tennessee border), at Oochgelogy, and in present-day Gordon County (begun in 1821). These missions were successful until the federal removal policy (Trail of Tears) led to their closures in the 1830s. Today, the Moravian presence and influence in Georgia is found in a single Moravian congregation at Stone Mountain.

This monument was presented to the city of Savannah by the Wachovia Historical Society, the oldest historical society in North Carolina. They are dedicated to the preservation of Moravian Society. The Moravians fled religious persecution in Czechoslovakia, only to encounter resistance here in America, too. Though their first settlement started in North America, in Savannah, was unsuccessful, they eventually found a home in this new world. Today, they number 60,000 in the United States and over a million worldwide.

Wesley Monument: The Whole World Is My Parish

John and Charles Wesley were young and a bit guileless when they came to America as clergy for the Church of England. Their trip here, a four-month voyage, would set John on a course that would eventually lead to his founding of the Methodist Church. It was on the

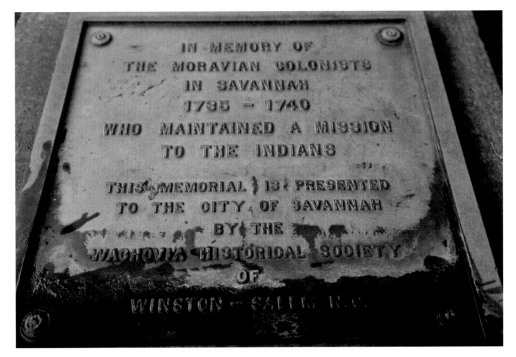

Close-up of the plaque of the Moravian Monument.

The John Wesley Monument.

ship over that two important events happened for John. He encountered the Moravians and a woman by the name of Sophia Hopkey. The Moravians would lead to a change in his heart, and Miss Hopkey would lead him to a quick exit from Georgia.

During the trip, the Moravians and their prayer life and confidence in their fate would call John's own faith into question. One incident exemplifies the Moravians. John's ship faced a terrible storm. While the English panicked, the Moravians stayed calm and composed. They sang hymns and prayed. The contrast made John believe that the Moravians possessed an inner strength he craved.[118] The Moravians came to Savannah seeking religious freedom and a worldwide missionary effort to unite people of all faiths. John attended a Moravian meeting, in which he heard a reading of Luther's preface to the Epistle to the Romans and was moved by the experience.

The Moravians were pious people whose heartfelt religion and communal living challenged John's academic and clerical religion. Many believed this encounter with the Moravians was the event that led to the "conversion experience" of his heart being strangely warmed at a church in Aldersgate, England. The strangely warmed heart would lead John to formulate a new denomination separate from the Church of England.

Sophia Hopkey would be another matter of the heart, but this one did not have the desired result. On the voyage over, John was asked to tutor Hopkey in French. During these

Wesley depicted with an open Bible, preaching.

Side view of the Wesley Monument.

on numerous occasions. And to make matters worse, Thomas Causton, the uncle of Sophia, challenged Wesley to fight in a duel.

Wesley, determined to explain, wrote a letter to Sophie's husband. In it he declared that she had a matter she needed to confess in front of the congregation before he could administer the Communion. He also said she had not been to church in months and had not made the customary notice to the curate of her intention the day before. Concluding the letter, he wrote these were the reasons he had not allowed her to participate in the sacrament. None of this was found satisfactory to her husband and Wesley soon found himself in court. Various juries and judges repeatedly were unable to agree to a verdict. The event was so divisive that one trustee was sent to investigate the incident. He was convinced that Wesley was devout, but not necessarily right. The controversy lasted three years: from June 25, 1750, to July 27, 1753.[120]

lessons and the long journey, they exchanged vows of love. The relationship continued for a while after they landed in Savannah, but John conferred with a Moravian minister who told him a commitment to marriage would hamper his commitment to minister to the inhabitants of Georgia. John, taking this advice, called off the "engagement." On March 12, 1737, Sophia Hopkey married William Williamson, a clerk in her uncle's store. The marriage seemed to disturb John (who probably felt she should not marry anyone, although he had broken off with her). Wesley's

hurt was seemingly expressed when, on August 7, 1737, he refused to give Mrs. Williamson Holy Communion at a church service. This did not set well with Sophie and her new husband, so the following day, they issued a warrant against Wesley. The warrant claimed Wesley had damaged their reputation with his refusal of Communion. When brought before the court, Wesley claimed it was a church matter and not a state matter and, therefore, he did not have to answer.[119] It was at this time that rumors were spreading that Wesley had had his marriage proposals rebuffed

Meanwhile, in Frederica, a small fort town south of Savannah, Charles was having his own lady problems. Two women of questionable reputations had a fight for Charles' affections. The incident caused General Oglethorpe to have a lack of confidence in the man. To discipline this, Wesley Oglethorpe stripped him of his bed, to force him to sleep on the ground, and allowed him only the basic necessities. John had to intervene and ask for Charles to be able to have a bed and another chance. On a visit to Ft. Frederica, he found the spiritual life appalling. John also found one of the aforementioned women, who then tried to shoot him. A scuffle ensued and finally others arrived to remove her. Charles left for England shortly thereafter in August 1736.[121]

Back in Savannah, John was under continuing legal pressure and his reputation was suffering, so he left the following year in December 1737. Though his stay in Georgia was filled with frontier and small town excitement, his time in Savannah influenced John greatly. The seeds of a new denomination were planted in his heart here.

Today, there are over 70 million Methodists worldwide. The United Methodist Church is the third largest Christian denomination. John Wesley is considered one of the great preachers and theologians of the Christian church.

The monument on Reynolds Square was erected by the Methodists of Georgia, in 1969, to honor John Wesley. It is on the site where his home and gardens are believed to have been. It depicts Wesley at age thirty-three in a preaching stance and made of black marble. It was created by Marshall Daugherty, a professor at Mercer University in Macon, Georgia, and also the son of a Methodist minister. Daugherty would become a noted regional artist, doing a sculpture of Pan at the Macon Science and Arts Museum, a bust of author Harry Stillwell Edwards for the Macon Public Library, and he designed the ceremonial mace for Mercer University, where he headed the Art Department. The Wesley Monument would be the only project of this size that Daugherty would ever create.

At the base of the statue are two quotes from Wesley himself. The first, "While we live, let us live in earnest." And secondly, "I look upon all the world as my parish." Methodism has three "general rules" that originated with the Wesleys; not rules for achieving salvation but, rather, for putting faith into practice. These, in shorthand form, are:

1. Do all the good you can.
2. Avoid evil.
3. Attend the ordinances of God, which include prayer, worship attendance, Bible reading, and fasting.

On the issue of wealth and material goods, John Wesley had a three-part approach:

1. Earn all you can.
2. Save all you can.
3. Give all you can.

Wesley, the elder statesman and founder of Methodism, never accepted any more money than what he had earned in seminary and could be found at the age of eighty walking door to door through a foot of snow collecting alms for the poor. Despite his early troubles in Savannah, he became a devout man who chose the world as his parish and found a method to promote a spirituality that has been practiced by many for two centuries.

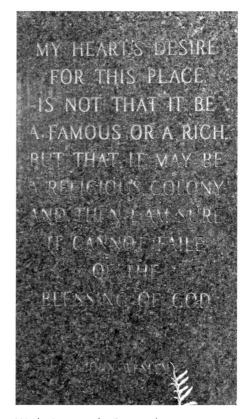

Wesley's prayer for Savannah.

V

FARTHER AFIELD

Sidewalk into the Yamacraw Art Project.

Yamacraw Public Art Project:
We All Have A Story To Tell

Leadership Savannah was formed in 1961 to educate leaders about the various programs and issues facing the Savannah area. Through talking to government, non-profits, and other organizations, the participants of Leadership Savannah hopefully obtain the information to make them better future leaders. Each class consists of forty-two members and, at the end of the class, typically they've developed a project. The initial idea for the Yamacraw Public Art Project came from two Leadership Savannah participants: Susan Watts and Terry Pindar. But the project would take fourteen years to complete and the leaders of the project would change until it became a community undertaking. The idea for the project was to select a part of the city that did not usually have art displayed, and then to create an artistic work. For the location, a "square" in front of the Bryan Street Baptist Church, in the middle of a

Statues of children playing in the fountain at the Yamacraw Art Project.

The historic First Bryan Baptist Church that sits by the park with the Yamacraw Art Project.

government housing project called Yamacraw Village, was chosen.

The location was essential to the artistic concept that was developed. The site was probably the location of Tomochichi's tribe and remnants of the Native American heritage can still found in the name of the village, Yamacraw. But the area also was in front of the church founded by Andrew Bryan. Bryan, a unique individual and powerful minister, started the historic First African Baptist Church, the oldest slave church in America, found on Franklin Square. It was a church built by the slave parishioners after their work

was completed for their masters. The church had a doctrinal dispute in 1832 and the Bryan Street Baptist Church was formed by the group who left. Both churches rightfully claim Andrew Bryan as their founder.

Jerome Meadows was chosen as the artist for the project by the project committee. Meadows was born in the Bronx. His major public sculptures include the Martin Luther King Jr. Living Memorial in Anchorage, Alaska; *Truths That Rise From Roots Remembered* in Alexandria, Virginia; *To Create the Beloved Community* in Albuquerque, New Mexico; and *Carry the Rainbow on Your Shoulders* in Washington, DC.

Meadows moved to Savannah in 1997 when he accepted a commission to design and create the Yamacraw Public Art Park. Meadows' heritage includes both African-American and Native American (Cherokee) ancestors. He also knew how it was to grow up in an inner city environment. Meadows, after moving to Savannah, opened one of the city's most innovative art galleries in the Eastside Neighborhood called Indigo Sky. He now calls Savannah home and is a leader in the local art community.[122]

Meadows elected, as the centerpiece of the park sculptures, three children who look as though they are playing in the water of the fountain he designed. The project cost $337,000 and took fourteen years to complete. The project makes one hope that Leadership Savannah never loses the knowledge of Savannah's heritage or the inclusion of all, especially children, in the aspirations, opportunities, and attainments of our community.[123]

Historic First Bryan Baptist Church.

Spring Hill Redoubt Marker: The Bold and Beautiful

Surrounded by one of Savannah's greatest historic economic enterprises sits this small monument to a great Revolutionary War battle: the Central of Georgia Railroad and Canal Company, chartered in 1833. The battlefield was the scene of one of the bloodiest engagements in that War. Eight hundred colonial soldiers were wounded or killed here. Concrete squares show how the soldiers neared the redoubt that stood before them. In lines of ten they approached the fortified embankments of the British. At some point they charged at breakneck speed, all the time

The Spring Hill Redoubt Monument in Battlefield Park.

trying to hold their lines. The British stood behind the fortifications, firing and defending their position. The rebels, try as they might, could not sustain a breach in the British lines. Briefly, at three different times, openings were created. Once, the regimental flag, planted to help direct other soldiers to the breach, fell. The gallant Sergeant Jasper leaped into the narrowing void to lift the flag so that his fellow soldiers could follow through the small hole they had created in the British defense. But it was a British day, as Jasper was shot,

The flag at Battlefield Park.

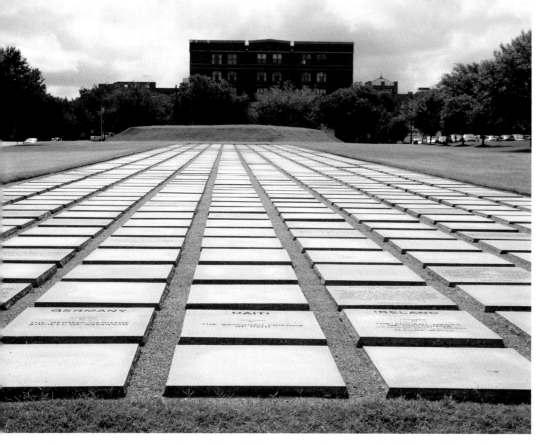

Concrete squares representing soldiers in formation as they approached the British redoubt.

killed, and taken from the battlefield. Another breach formed, but then it too quickly closed. Count Casimir Pulaski saw the British filling this gap. He charged ahead on his stallion, determined that he and his men would not allow the break to vanish. Pulaski was mortally wounded and carried off the battlefield. The colonial soldiers had lost. The brave Haitians stepped up and held the charging British back as the defeated troops fled. Their courage saved many American lives that day. Savannah would stay in British hands until after the Yorktown surrender.

Outside of Savannah and Georgia, many have not heard of this battle. Maybe this is because the battle was a defeat and we are not a people who like defeat. Battles such as these remind us of the cost of war and that not every one is won. Bravery and heroism are found on both sides of a conflict. Even when we have superior numbers we may not win. Yet, this battle, with soldiers from all over Europe and other places, shows that there was a united cry from men who believed there are certain inalienable rights and that we are created equal before the law. That cry is still heard and shared by people all over the world, even when we do not always live up to that vision. But the cry should be embedded in our hearts and minds and our feet as we walk forward into the same dream to which hearts beat so long ago.

Bishop Turner Monument: "I Claim the Rights of a Man"

Tucked just a little way outside of the Historic District, across from the Savannah College of Art and Design Museum of Art, is a monument to one of the United States' most prominent nineteenth-century African-Americans: Bishop Henry McNeal Turner. The monument is placed at the site where Turner served as pastor of St. Philip AME Church (now known at St. Philip Monumental AME Church) from 1870 to 1874. St. Philip Monumental, the "Mother Church of African Methodism in Georgia," was organized here on June 16, 1865.

Turner was born a freeman in Abbeville, South Carolina, on February 1, 1834, and died on May 5, 1915. The eighty-one years of his life were one of America's remarkable stories.

His religious career was significant because of the many AME churches he started after the Civil War. During the Civil War, he was named the first black chaplain in the United States Army in 1863. He primarily served the First Regiment of United States Colored Troops, a regiment he helped create and for which he recruited soldiers. Turner was elected Bishop of Georgia AME churches in 1880.

Turner may be considered as the

Bishop Henry McNeal Turner Monument.

BISHOP HENRY McNEAL TURNER
1834 - 1915

Henry McNeal Turner was the first Black Chaplain of the U.S. Army. He was appointed by President Lincoln in 1863.

In 1865, he was assigned an agent of the Freedmen's Bureau in Georgia.

He served in the Georgia House of Representatives from 1868-1870; and at one time was postmaster of Macon.

Turner served as pastor of St. Phillips A.M.E. Church in Savannah (now known as St. Philip Monumental A.M.E. Church) from 1870-1874. St. Philip Monumental, the "Mother Church of African Methodism in Georgia", was organized on this site, June 18, 1865.

Turner was elected Bishop of Georgia in 1880. Bishop Turner was prominent in the back-to-Africa movement, leading two expeditions from the Port of Savannah in the 1890's.

He was a pioneer in the establishment and expansion of missionary work in Africa.

precursor of the Black Liberation Theology Movement. In his sermons, he often stated that God was a negro, a phrase meant to show God's unique concern for blacks (a concept shocking even today). In 1885, showing his well-known radicalness, he became the first AME bishop to ordain a woman, Sarah Ann Hughes, to the office of deacon.[124]

He was equally groundbreaking in his political career. Reverend Turner helped organize Georgia's Republican Party and served in the state's new Constitutional Convention. He was elected to the Georgia House of Representatives to represent Macon, becoming one of the first black legislators in America. His term was cut short with the assassination of President Abraham Lincoln and the revocation of many of the reforms of Reconstruction. In 1868, the vast majority of white legislators decided to expel their African-American peers on the grounds that holding public office was a privilege denied blacks. When the Georgia legislature was voting on whether to seat the newly elected black legislators, Reverend Turner delivered a speech, "Am I Not a Man," that is still recognized as one of America's greatest speeches. A quote from the speech reads:

> Mr. Speaker: Before proceeding
> to argue this question upon
> its intrinsic merits, I wish the
> members of this House to
> understand the position that I
> take. I hold that I am a member
> of this body. Therefore, sir, I
> shall neither fawn nor cringe
> before any party, nor stoop to

St. Philips Monumental AME Church, where Bishop Turner was pastor while in Savannah.

beg them for my rights. Some of my colored fellow members, in the course of their remarks, took occasion to appeal to the sympathies of members on the opposite side, and to eulogize their character for magnanimity. It reminds me very much, sir, of slaves begging under the lash. I am here to demand my rights and to hurl thunderbolts at the men who would dare to cross the threshold of my manhood. There is an old aphorism which says, "Fight the devil with fire," and if I should observe the rule in this instance, I wish gentlemen to understand that it is but fighting them with their own weapon.[125]

Though his eloquence was unmatched, the black legislators would eventually be unseated.

Turner's politics matched his activism. He was angered by the pre-Civil War white power structure regaining power and instituting Jim Crow laws. Turner began to support Black Nationalism and emigration of blacks to Africa, a concept that would plant ideas for Marcus Garvey and Malcolm X in the twentieth century. He owned two newspapers: *The Voice of Missions* (he served as editor from 1893 to 1900) and later *The Voice of the People* (editor from 1901 to 1904). These newspapers helped him found the International Migration Society, an effort to move blacks from the United States back to Africa where they could find equality in economics, political, and social spheres. He organized two ships that left the Savannah harbor with a total of 500 or more emigrants, who traveled to Liberia in 1895 and 1896. In the typical "you cannot go home again" experience, many of the migrants chose to return to America after dealing with the British colonist control system in Liberia.[126] Turner did not continue these efforts.

Although Turner was a pioneer in many of his activities, he never saw some of his significant dreams come to pass: voters' rights laws, civil rights legislation, and a black president among them. But he was a proud voice crying in the wilderness of Georgia and Savannah many years before black mayors, black uncontested state representatives, and black council members could be found. In this monument we are reminded to appreciate our new voices in the wilderness.

Jasper Springs Monument: Springing Into Action

There are few non-commissioned officers who are honored with a monument. Usually, monuments are dedicated to the generals, officers, or other leaders. Yet Sergeant Jasper has three. He also has counties and parks that bear his name. The Jasper Springs Monument commemorates one of his military achievements. It was here with cohort Sergeant John Newton that he ambushed ten British soldiers and freed several American fighters who were being transported to Savannah. The legend and history of Jasper was popularized by Parson Weems in his various books on the heroes of the Revolutionary War. This influential early historian is where one can find the story of George Washington chopping down the cherry tree and his refusal to tell a lie about it. Weems wrote his books in the early nineteenth century to honor the heroes of the Revolutionary War and offer moral instruction to its readers. Obviously, Weems thought the character and stories of Jasper were worth instruction and keeping in the American mythos.

This particular monument was erected in 1937 by the United States government, before the viaduct was in place that now surrounds it. The spring is seldom, if at all, running these days. The monument is seldom visited, primarily because it is difficult to find. Jasper was illiterate and a commoner, but he has left his mark in his new country. This and the other two monuments to this non-commissioned officer remind us of the American value of equality for all.

Jasper Springs Monument. Notice the covering over the springs in the background.

A close-up of Jasper Springs Monument plaque.

Cohen Humane Drinking Fountain: All Creatures Great and Small

Percival Randolph Cohen was the CEO of the Savannah Compress Company. He was also to become a significant Savannah philanthropist, leaving $50,000 in his will to build Cohen's Old Man's Retreat, a thirty-one bed home for elderly men; he also left $63,000 to the Bethesda Home for Boys, to build one of their residential homes named Cohen Cottage. Cohen left a gift of $40,000 to the Froebel Circle, named after the founder of the kindergarten movement, German Frederick Froebel. The group was founded by local innovative educator

Cohen Humane Fountain now stands in the middle of Victory Drive.

and activist Nina Pape. The work of the Circle was to be directed toward increasing the health and happiness of underprivileged children. This gift made it possible for the Circle to erect a building known as the Cohen Shelter for Little Ones on Tybee Island. On April 15, 1929, the cornerstone, that included a box containing corn, wine, and oil, emblematic of plenty, the spirit of joy, and the spirit of peace, was laid. The box also contained a copy of the *Savannah Morning News*, a copy of Mr. Cohen's will, a history of the Froebel Circle, a coin of the year 1898, and a coin of

Cohen Humane Fountain. The top is designed as a birdbath and the lower is a trough for horses to drink from.

the year 1928.[127] The summer camp for needy children is still active today.

Cohen also left $1,500 in his will to the city of Savannah for a drinking fountain for horses and mules that were the workhorses for transporting cotton. One can imagine he often watched the horses on hot days trudging along and felt compassion for them. The only problem was that when he included the fountain in his will and, by the time he died, things had changed. We were quickly moving into an automobile culture and horses and mules were to be found on farms, but not urban areas. The city hired one of its best architects, Henrik Wallin, to design the fountain. He'd designed various buildings around town including the Armstrong House (which would become the birthplace of Armstrong Atlantic State University), the Savannah College of Art and Design's Wallin Hall, and the major renovation and redesign of First Baptist Church to name three. To solve the problem of the fountain for animals that were no longer seen on the streets of Savannah, he designed it with a birdbath on top and water for dogs underneath. Initially, the Fountain stood in the middle of the wide, brick-paved intersection of Bay and Whitaker Streets. But in 1945, as automobile traffic increased, the city moved the Fountain to Victory Drive and Bull Street.[128]

Through his will, Cohen cared for the less fortunate. His will offered respite for the old, the orphaned, and impoverished children. The concept of taking under-privileged children to the beach for two weeks to experience the benefits of fresh air, exercise, and

the beauty of nature was innovative for that time. Remarkably, Cohen's mandate also included a gift to the animals. And one could infer from its title Cohen Humane Fountain he thought it humane to include the animals in our concerns and care. Today, many thousands pass this gift for work animals everyday, but few will know the heart of the man who gave it to Savannah.

World War I Monument: Victory Was Ours

The state of Georgia had more training camps during World War I than any other state. By the end of the War, 100,000 men and women from Georgia had participated in training. Even though the war officially ended with the signing of the Treaty of Versailles, on June 28, 1919, the final troops that had been deployed did not come home until May 30, 1923. They disembarked in Savannah.

So it should be of no surprise that Savannah celebrated this war with a memorial. Savannahians commemorated the war effort through two things. The

Victory Drive.

first was by changing the name of Estill Avenue to Victory Drive in 1919, adding over nineteen miles to the east and west. Savannah landscaped the newly named road with palm trees and azaleas in the median that divided the road. Over 360 palm trees and 350 azaleas were planted

The World War I Monument.

The pond and fountain in Daffin Park.

The circle for turning around carriages at the end of the promenade of the lawn of oak trees designed by John Nolen.

in honor of the soldiers of World War I. The road became one of the most scenic roads in America.

The second thing Savannah did was create a monument to the men from Chatham County who had died in the War. It stands seven feet by six feet. It was originally placed in the median of Victory Drive, but it was decided that no one could see the Monument in that location and it was moved into historic Daffin Park. Daffin Park is one of Savannah's jewels. It was designed by noted American landscape architect John Nolen. Nolen's design would reflect his genius and can be seen also in Balboa Park, San Diego, California; Wisconsin's first four state parks; and Independence Park in Charlotte, North Carolina; to name a few.

The monument can now be easily seen and approached. That is important because on the monument are these words, "They do not die who serve humanity." The beauty of Victory Drive and Daffin Park belies the blood spilled in war, but they are also reminders of the quality of life the soldiers fought to preserve.

Landscaping around World War I Monument.

The back of the World War I Monument.

EPILOGUE

Some of the untold stories of Savannah's monuments now have been shared, but the stories can never be completely told. New monuments will come, new information will be unveiled, and monuments will take on different interpretations at different periods of history. Think of how the Lincoln Memorial, in Washington, DC, developed a deeper meaning after Martin Luther King Jr. delivered his "I Have a Dream" speech at its steps.

The possibilities of future monuments abound. The gay community, Asian, and Latino have all made contributions to our community, but currently no monument exists representative of these communities. Savannah has also had a cadre of strong and important women and, currently, only a monument to Florence Martus exists.

The Waving Girl is one of the great iconic images of Savannah. She stands with towel in hand welcoming all to Savannah's safe harbor. But she also stands as a reminder that monuments can come from unusual and unexpected places. The creative telling of Savannah's history has only begun and new takes and creative acts will occur, old ones will be remembered or discovered. They will call us to capture a moment we do not want to see lost.

Eventually, all of these groups will, deservingly so, want to be represented by a monument in the fabric of the city. Yet real estate, especially prime locations, for these monuments are becoming less available. We know population trends are changing and minority populations are growing. A city has to make room to include all of its history and communities in the telling of their stories. A great city will provide the literal space in their fabric to tell all its stories or the city will not be fully whole and its history will have significant gaps in it.

It is late. The stories have been told, the children have been put to sleep, and the adults are finally ready for bed. The dreams of the community await. The memories of the good and bad of the past and the hopes and visions of the future are ever near. Good night and have sweet dreams.

APPENDIX

Map 1

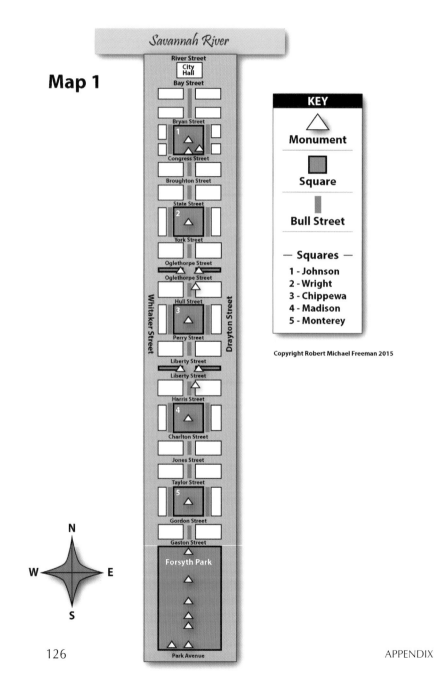

Walking Tours of the Monuments

I have included a four-part tour guide map, along with GPS coordinates and addresses for the monuments that are farther afield. The book is coordinated with the four tours. If one were to walk all four parts of the tour of the monuments, they would have walked approximately six miles.

The first tour includes what we have labeled as the Avenue of Heroes. It starts at a grand promenade from the south of Forsyth Park to City Hall. This tour has some of the oldest and grandest monuments of Savannah. It is approximately 1.3 miles long. At City Hall, located on the west or left side next to the back of the building, is an elevator. To begin the River Street tour, take the elevator down to River Street to the African-American Monument.

126

The River Street Tour, if you are continuing from the Avenue of Heroes, starts by going west, or left, if you are facing the African-American Monument. After the Steamship of Savannah Monument, you would return to the African-American Monument and continue down River Street.

River Street today is a tourist mecca with old cotton warehouses filled with shops, bars, and restaurants. In the past it has been where the slaves, Oglethorpe, Savannah Jews, Moravians, Salzburgers, and others first set foot in America. It is where the *Steamship Savannah* launched and Liberty Ships for War World II were made. It has the renowned *Waving Girl*, World War II Monument, and Olympic Torch Monument, as well as others. It was the original port of Savannah. The River Street Tour is a little less than a mile.

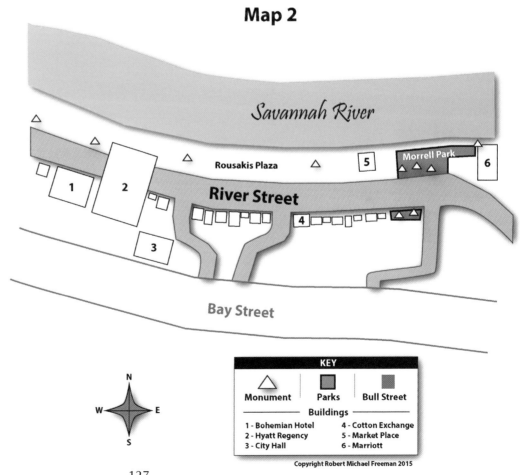

Map 2

Savannah River

Rousakis Plaza

Morrell Park

River Street

Bay Street

KEY		
Monument	Parks	Bull Street

— Buildings —

1 - Bohemian Hotel   4 - Cotton Exchange
2 - Hyatt Regency   5 - Market Place
3 - City Hall   6 - Marriott

Copyright Robert Michael Freeman 2015

Map 3

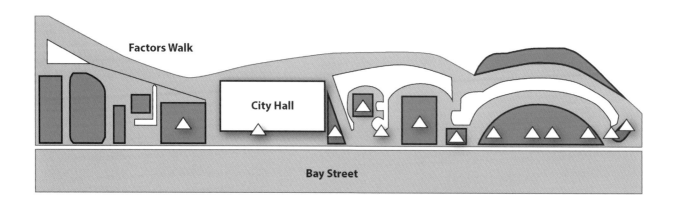

Copyright Robert Michael Freeman 2015

The Bay Street Tour, if you are continuing from the River Street Tour, is accessed by a steep stairway up to Emmett Park or a walk on the cobblestone River Street access road to Emmett Park. These are found next to Morrell Park. The Bay Street Tour starts at the eastern end of Emmett Park at the Old Harbor Light. It continues from the Old Harbor Light west, staying on the north side of Bay Street and ending with the Oglethorpe Bench. This tour includes the Vietnam War Memorial, Salzburger Monument, Washington Guns, Cotton Exchange Griffin, and many other monuments. Factors Walk runs parallel to Bay Street and is where wagons full of cotton would travel under the various walkways, and "factors" would call out prices they would give to the cotton shown beneath them. Bay Street is home to the Cotton Exchange and City Hall. This tour is one half of a mile.

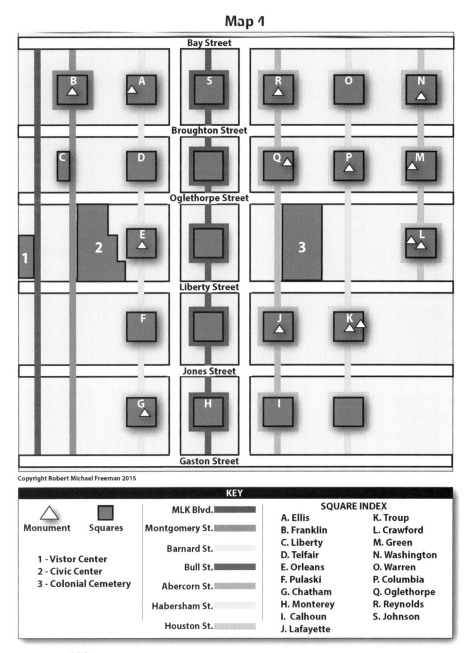

Map 1

Copyright Robert Michael Freeman 2015

The final tour is the Other Monument Tours. It travels through most of the squares not located on Bull Street. If you are finishing the Bay Street Tour and want to continue into this tour you would cross Bay Street at Barnard Street and continue at Ellis Square at the Johnny Mercer Statue. Otherwise you would start in Ellis Square. This is the longest tour but includes some of Savannah's most significant monuments such as the Haitian and Wesley Monuments; this tour also takes you for a stroll through Savannah's beautiful squares. To follow this map, start with the letter A (Ellis Square) and follow alphabetically until you reach the letter S (Johnson Square). This tour is approximately 3.3 miles.

KEY		
Monument △ Squares ▢	MLK Blvd. ▬ Montgomery St. ▬ Barnard St. ▬ Bull St. ▬ Abercorn St. ▬ Habersham St. ▬ Houston St. ▬	**SQUARE INDEX**

1 - Vistor Center
2 - Civic Center
3 - Colonial Cemetery

SQUARE INDEX

A. Ellis	K. Troup
B. Franklin	L. Crawford
C. Liberty	M. Green
D. Telfair	N. Washington
E. Orleans	O. Warren
F. Pulaski	P. Columbia
G. Chatham	Q. Oglethorpe
H. Monterey	R. Reynolds
I. Calhoun	S. Johnson
J. Lafayette	

Monuments Located Outside the Historic District

The monuments included here are outside of the Historic District. Some are within walking distance of the Historic District; others are not. We have included the addresses and GPS coordinates for them.

Yamacraw Art Project
> 565 West Bryan Street between
>   Bay Street and Bryan Street
> N 32 04.947
> W 081 05.931
> 17s E487926   N3549578

Spring Hill Redoubt Marker
> Found in Battlefield Park.
>   Corner of Martin Luther King, Jr. Boulevard
>   and Louisville Road.
> N 32 04.558
> W 08 06.023
> 17s E490526   N354880

Jasper Springs Monument
> Found on Augusta Avenue opposite
>   of the on-ramp for I-516.
> N 32 05.382
> W 081 07.677
> 17s E 487926   W 3550385

Bishop Turner Monument
> Found near the intersection of Fahm St.
>   And Turner Blvd. across from
>   the SCAD Museum of Art.

Cohen Humane Fountain
> Found in median at Bull Street and Victory
>   Drive. Designed in 1934 by Henrik Wallin

World War I Monument
> Found in Daffin Park on the northwest corner
>   at the intersection of Waters Avenue
>   and Victory Drive.

Alphabetical Listing of Monuments

I have listed all of the monuments and some pertinent information below in alphabetical order. A monument is generally defined for the purposes of this book as a built structure with information about an event, person, place, or thing. All monuments can be found in the Historic District unless mentioned in the Farther Afield section of book.

African-American Monument, 2002
> Sculpted by Dorothy Spradley
> Located on River Street

Anchor Monument, 1974
> Unknown artist
> Located on River Street
> Commissioned/funded by the Savannah
>   Chapter of the Women's Propeller Club

Armillary, 1968
> Designed by Kenneth Lynch & Sons
> Located in Troup Square
> Commissioned by Mills B. Lane
>   and Anna Waring Lane

Bartow and McLaws Busts, 1903
> Sculpted by George Julian Zolnay (1863-1949)
> Located originally in Chippewa Square,
>   now in Forsyth Park
> Funded by the city of Savannah;
>   Savannah Confederate Veterans Association

Big Duke Alarm Bell, 1985
> Unknown artist
> Located in the median of Oglethorpe
>   and Abercorn Streets
> Funded by the city of Savannah; Chatham
>   County Firefighters Memorial Committee
> Obelisk, purchased 1870s

British Evacuation Marker, 1904
> Unknown artist
> Located in Forsyth Park
> Funded by Lachlan McIntosh; DAR

Bull Sundial, 1933
> Unknown artist
> Located in Johnson Square
> Funded by the Society of Colonial Wars

Button Gwinnett Monument, 1964
> Designed by Ben Ritzert
> Located in Colonial Cemetery
> Funded by the Georgia Society of the SAR;
>   DAR; American Revolution Society of
>   Colonial Wars; Colonial Dames of America;
>   Savannah-Chatham Historic Site and
>   Monument Commission

Chatham Artillery Monument, 1986
> Unknown artist
> Located in Emmett Park

Cisterns Marker, n.d.
> Designed by Amos Scudder, William Clusky
>   created cistern in 1830s
> Located in Crawford Square

City Hall Fountain, 1906
> Sculpted by Fernando Miranda y Casellas
>   (1842-1925)
> Located inside City Hall
> Funded by city of Savannah

Cohen Humane Fountain, 1934
> Designed by Henrik Wallin (active early 1900s)
> Located in the median of Victory Street
> Funded by Randolph Percival Cohen;
>   Louisa King; ASPCA

Colonial Road Markers, 1920
> Unknown artist
> Located on Madison Square
> Funded by Savannah DAR

Confederate Memorial, 1879
> Designed by Robert Reid, Confederate soldier
>   sculpted by David Richards
> Located in Forsyth Park
> Funded by Ladies Memorial Association

Cotton Exchange, 1889
> Unknown artist
> Located on Bay Street

Crawford Square Recreation Monument, 2010
Unknown artist
Located in Crawford Square
Funded by Crawford Square
Alumni Association

Desoto Monument, 1992
Designed by Billy Nelson (sculptor)
and Allen Mason (artist)
Located on River Street behind Marriott Inn
Funded by Armstrong Atlanta State University
Hispanic Society

Flame of Freedom, 1969
Unknown artist
Located at Montgomery and York Streets
Funded by city of Savannah; Veterans of
Georgia; Chatham County; Chatham Post
36; Savannah Post 135; Cherokee Post 154;
George K. Gaman 184

Forsyth Park Fountain, 1858
Designed by Jacques Ignace Hittorff
Located in Forsyth Park

Georgia Hussars Memorial, 1960
Unknown artist
Located on Bay Street
Funded by Military Commission

Georgia Volunteer, 1931
Sculpted by Theo Kitson (1871-1932)
Located in Forsyth Park
Funded by United Spanish War Veterans

German Memorial, 1989
Unknown artist
Located on Orleans Square
Funded by German Heritage Society; German
Friendly Society; Georgia Salzburger Society

Gordon Monument, 1883
Designed by H. Van Brunt (1832-1903) and
Frank Howe (1849-1909)
Located in Wright Square
Funded by Central Railroad and
Banking Company of Georgia

Greene Monument, 1825
Designed by William Strickland (1788-1854)
Located in Johnson Square
Funded by People of Savannah

Haitian Monument, 2007
Sculpted by James Mastin
Located in Franklin Square
Funded by Haitian American Historical Society

International Seaman's House Bell, 2007
Unknown artist
Located on Washington Square
Funded by Propeller Club;
Port of Savannah Club

Irish Monument, 1983
Designed by Cathal Cragg
Located in Emmett Park
Funded by Savannah Irish
Monument Committee

Jasper Monument, 1888
Sculpted by Alexander Doyle (1857-1922)
Located in Madison Square
Funded by Jasper Memorial Association

Jasper Springs Monument, 1937
Unknown artist
Located on Augusta Avenue
Funded by United States Government

Jewish Burial Monument, 1983
Unknown artist
Located in the median between Oglethorpe
and Bull Streets
Funded by Mordecai Sheftall Cemetery Trust

Jones, Noble Wimberly Bust, 2004
Sculpted by Kevin Conlon (active early 2000s)
Located in Emmett Park
Funded by Georgia Medical Society

Korean War Monument, 2006
Unknown artist
Located in Emmett Park

Liberty Ship Marker, n.d.
Unknown artist
Located in Morrell Park
Funded by Sons of the Revolution
in the State of Georgia

Lion's Club Memorial, 1981
Unknown artist
Located in Morrell Park
Funded by Savannah Lion's Club

Marine Corps Monument, 1947
Unknown artist
Located in Forsyth Park
Funded by Savannah Detachment
Marine Corps League

Mercer Bench, 2003
Unknown artist
Located in Johnson Square
Funded by Johnny Mercer Foundation

Mercer Statue, 2009
Sculpted by Susie Chisholm (active 2000s)
Located in Ellis Square
Funded by Friends of Johnny Mercer

Moravian Monument, 1933
Unknown artist
Located in Oglethorpe Square
Funded by Wachovia Historical Society
of Winston-Salem

Myers Drinking Fountain, 1888 (in Forsyth Park)
Unknown artist (reconstructed by Ivan Bailey)
Located in Troup Square
Funded by city of Savannah

Oglethorpe Bench, 1906
Designed by Julian de Buryn Kops
Located on Bay Street
Funded by Colonial Dames Savannah Chapter

Oglethorpe Monument, 1910
Sculpted by Daniel Chester French (1850-1931)
Located in Chippewa Square
Funded by State of Georgia;
city of Savannah and others

Old City Exchange Bell, 1957 (purchased 1802)
Unknown artist
Located on Bay Street
Funded by/tower erected by Chamber of
Commerce; Pilot Clubs; Savannah-Chatham
Historic Site and Monument Commission

Old Harbor Light, 1858
Unknown artist
Located in Emmett Park

Olympic Torch Monument, 1996
    Designed by Ivan Bailey
        (active 1980s to present)
    Located in Morrell Park
    Funded by Savannah Foundation;
        city of Savannah

Peace Pole, n.d.
    Unknown artist
    Located in Morrell Park

Police Officers' Monument,
1982 (base erected 1964)
    Wooden model carved by G.W. Woods
    Located in median between Oglethorpe
        and Habersham Streets
    Funded by Police Officers' Wives Association

Pulaski Monument, 1853
    Designed by Robert Launitz (1806-1870)
    Located in Monterey Square
    Funded by Pulaski Monument Commission

Rotary Club Monument,
1925 (at bridge; moved in 1970s)
    Unknown artist
    Located in median between Liberty
        and Bull Streets
    Funded by Rotary Club of Savannah

St. Andrews Monument, 1987
    Unknown artist
    Located in median between Oglethorpe
        and Bull Streets
    Funded by Saint Andrews Society of Savannah

Salzburger Monument, 1994
    Designed by Anton Thuswaldner
    Located in Salzburger Park on Bay Street
    Funded by Salzburger Monument Committee;
        Government of Austria

Second African Baptist Church, 1976
    Unknown artist
    Located on Greene Square
    Funded by city of Savannah

Semiquincentenary Monument, 1983
    Unknown artist
    Located in Lafayette Square
    Funded by National Society
        of the Colonial Dames

Southern Line of Defenses Monument, 1929
    Unknown artist
    Located in Madison Square
    Funded by city of Savannah; Patriotic Society

Spring Hill Redoubt Monument, 2007
    Unknown artist
    Located in Battlefield Park
    Funded by Sons of Revolution Georgia

Steamship Savannah Monument, 1992
    Unknown artist
    Located on River Street
    Funded by Propeller Club

Tomochichi Monument, 1899
    Unknown artist
    Located in Wright Square
    Funded by Georgia Society of Colonial Dames

Toomer Monument, 1964
    Unknown artist
    Located on Martin Luther King, Jr. Boulevard
        (Carver State Bank)

Toonahowie Birdbath, 1929
    Unknown artist
    Located on Bull Street between Hull
        and Oglethorpe Streets (in front of
        Board of Education building)
    Funded by Savannah Chapter of DAR

Turner Monument, 1987
    Unknown artist
    Located at 1112 Jefferson Street
        beside St. Philip Monumental AME
    Funded by AME Church
        Bicentennial Committee

Vietnam War Monument, 1991
    Designed by Matthew Dixon;
        peninsula carved by Jim Hudson
    Located in Emmett Park
    Funded by Chatham County Vietnam
        Veterans Memorial; city of Savannah

Washington Firehouse Marker, 2007
    Unknown artist
    Located in Washington Square

Washington Guns, 1791 (canons presented;
canopy built 1980s)
    Unknown artist
    Located on Bay Street

Waving Girl Monument, 1971
    Sculpted by Felix de Weldon (1907-2003)
    Located in Morrell Park
    Funded by Altrusa Club of Savannah

Wesley Monument, 1969
    Sculpted by Marshall Daughtery
    Located in Reynolds Square
    Funded by Methodists of Georgia;
        city of Savannah

World War I Monument, 1942
    Unknown artist
    Located in Daffin Park
    Funded by Savannah Women's Federation

World War II Monument, 2010
    Designed by Eric Meyerhoff;
        artist Kim Brandell
    Located on River Street
    Funded by Veteran's Council
        of Chatham County

Wormsloe Fountain, 1971
    Unknown artist
    Located in Columbia Square
    Funded by Savannah Park and Tree
        Department; Trustees Garden Club

Yamacraw Public Art Project, 2006
    Designed by Jerome Meadows
    Located in Yamacraw Village
    Funded by Yamacraw Public
        Art Project Committee

ENDNOTES

1 Gordon Smith, "The British Evacuate Savannah Georgia," *Sons of American Revolution Magazine* (Spring 2007).

2 Ibid.

3 Evan Thomas, *The War Lovers: Roosevelt, Lodge, Hearst and the Rush to Empire, 1898,* (New York: Back Bay Books/Little, Brown and Company, 2010) 276.

4 Charlotte Streifer Rubenstein, *American Women Artists,* (Boston: G.K. Holt, 1990) 102.

5 "Camille Claudel," New World Encyclopedia, May 6, 2008, www.newworldencyclopedia.org (accessed December 9, 2012).

6 Robert M. Poole, "How Arlington National Cemetery Came to Be," *Smithsonian Magazine* (November 2009).

7 Ibid.

8 Ibid.

9 United Daughters of the Confederacy, "Founder and Co-Founder," www.hqudc.org/ (accessed June 28, 2013).

10 Doug Gross, *Savannah Morning News,* April 27, 1998, http://savannahnow.com (accessed September 25, 2012).

11 Ron Freeman, *Savannah: People, Places, and Events* (Tallahassee, FL: Rose Printing Co., 2011) 45.

12 Todd W. Groce, "Francis S. Bartow (1816–1861)," *New Georgia Encyclopedia,* (accessed January 25, 2008.)

13 Kennedy Hickman, "American Revolution: Count Casimir Pulaski," About.com Military History (accessed November 3, 2012).

14 Margarita Venegas, "Pulaski Monument," www.georgiainfo.galileo.usg.edu.pulaskimon.htm (accessed February 2, 2012).

15 Edward Pinkowski, "General Pulaski's Body," presentation Pulaski Museum, Warka, Poland. October 1997, www.poles.org (accessed January 19, 2011).

16 Ibid.

17 Ibid.

18 Ibid.

19 Pamela Walck, "Pulaski Monument Rededicated," *Savannah Morning News,* October 10, 2001, (accessed February 4, 2013).

20 Michael Telzrow, "Ordinary Man, Extraordinary Hero: the story of Sergeant William Jasper is a reminder that ordinary men of extraordinary courage can shape history and inspire generations," American Opinion Publishing Inc., 2005.

21 Ibid.

22 Dorothy Stewart, *The Monuments and Foundations of Savannah: A Report on an Internship for the Savannah Park and Tree Department* (Dorothy Stewart, 1993).

23 Marcus Holland, "Sgt. Jasper one of their own, two groups say," Savannah Morning News, March 15, 1998, www.savannahnow.com (accessed January 5, 2013).

24 Ibid.

25 Rotary International Club, http://rotary.org/en/aboutus/history/pages/ridefault.aspx (accessed April 17, 2012).

26 Rotary Club of Savannah, www.sav.rotary.org (accessed June 19, 2012).

27 Stewart, 407.

28 Michael Thurmond, *Freedom: Georgia's Antislavery Heritage* (Atlanta: Longstreet Press, 2003), 19–20.

29 Ibid., 32.

30 "Encyclopedia of Southern Jewish Communities-Savannah, Georgia," www.isjl.org/georgia-savannah, 2006 (accessed April 19, 2012).

31 Elizabeth Cooksey, "Judaism and Jews," newgeorgiaencyclopedia.org, 11-30-07 (accessed April 18, 2012).

32 Ibid.

33 Ibid.

34 Ibid.

35 Ibid.

36 Elizabeth B. Cooksey, "Judaism and Jews in Georgia," www.georgiaencyclopedia.org (accessed March 3, 2009).

37 "A History of IPC—Independent Presbyterian Church," www.ipcasav.org (accessed June 9, 2013).

38 "A History of IPC—Independent Presbyterian Church," www.ipcasav.org (accessed June 9, 2013).

39 Charles Johnson, "William Washington Gordon (1796–1842)," www.georgiaencyclopedia.org, August 6, 2005 (accessed June 23, 2012).

40 Stewart, 366.

41 Ibid., 374.

42 Ibid., 374.

43 Terry Galway, *Washington's General: Nathaniel Greene and the Triumph of the American Revolution*, (New York: Henry Holt and Company, 2006), 40.

44 Ibid., 230.

45 Robert Middlekauff, *The Glorious Cause: The American Revolution, 1763-1789* (Oxford: Oxford University Press, 2005), 474.

46 Michael Kammen, *Digging Up the Dead: A History of Notable American Reburials* (Chicago: University of Chicago Press, 2010), 61.

47 Johnny Mercer Foundation, www.johnnymercerfoundation.org (accessed April 14, 2013).

48 David Gignilliant, "Gleaming Bench of Marble Accentuates the Positive," www.savannahbest.com, (accessed June 6, 2013).

49 Abigail Hester Williams Jordan, "Trials and Tribulations of Building an African-American Monument in Savannah, Georgia; 1991-2002," (Self-published, 2008) 1.

50 "19th Annual Consortium of Doctors to Induct a Parade of Stars July 24th," *Savannah Herald*, July 14, 2011.

51 Jordan, 8.

52 Brett Bell, "Council approves African-American Monument: After 10 years alderman decides to move forward with construction, but without controversial inscription," *Savannah Morning News*, January 12, 2001, www.savannahnow.com (accessed August 1, 2012).

53 "A Dream comes True: Savannah celebrates its newest monument, the first dedicated to African-Americans in a ceremony on River Street," *Savannah Morning News,* July 28, 2002, www.savannahnow.com (accessed August 1, 2012).

54 Tony Cope, "On the Swing Shift: Building Liberty Ships in Savannah," US Naval Blog, November, 2009 http://blog.usni.org/2009/11/16/on-the-swing-shift-building-liberty-ships-in-savannah-by-tony-cope (accessed January 13, 2012).

55 Ibid.

56 Jackie Heinz, The Zeigler House Inn, blog.zeiglerhouseinn.com (accessed February 19, 2011).

57 "Quotes of Savannah," www.pbase.com/savannahga/quotes (accessed June 27, 2013).

58 Chuck Mobley, "Commission to consider plan for WWII monument this week," *Savannah Morning News*, July 7, 2008, www.savannahnow.com (accessed September 4, 2012).

59 Ibid.

60 Lynda Figueredo, "World War II Monument takes shape in downtown Savannah," WTOC, October 18, 2010, www.wtoc.com (accessed June 10, 2012).

61 John Laurence Busch, *Steam Coffin: Moses Rogers and the Steamship Savannah Break the Barrier,* (Hodos Historian, 2010).

62 Ibid.

63 Ibid.

64 Ibid.

65 Mary Carr Mayle, "Remembering the NS Savannah," *Savannah Morning News*, August 23, 2012, www.savannahnow.com (accessed August 8, 2012).

66 "Capture of the Philippa 7-10-1775," American War of Independence at Sea, January 30, 2009 www.awaitsea.com (accessed March 8, 2012).

67 Ibid.

68 Lion's Club International, www.lionsclub.org (accessed May 1, 2013).

69 Erin Rossiter, "Savannah's monument to a maritime legend," Athens Banner-Herald, May 17, 2009, www.onlineathens.com (accessed June 19, 2012).

70 Ibid.

71 Elizabeth Carpenter Piechocinski, *Men of Iron, Men of Stone, Feet of Clay* (Savannah: Oglethorpe Press, 2006) 65-66.

72 Ivan Bailey, "Savannah Olympic Torch Sculpture," July 23, 1996, www.artmetal.com (accessed March 2, 2013).

73 Ibid.

74 Tommy McQueeny, "The Belle of Charleston's Renaissance—Elizabeth O'Neill Verner," Low Country Sun, June 1997, www.lowcountry.sun.com (accessed November 20, 2013).

75 William Harris Bragg, "Noble W. Jones (ca.1723–1805)," www.georgiaenclyopedia, September19, 2002 (accessed April 17, 2010).

76 Kevin Conlon: Online Portfolio, www.dl.dropboxusercontent.com/u/2154968/website/index.html (accessed May 8, 2013).

77 "Chatham Artillery Punch," www.Battleofolustee.org.punch.html (accessed June 1, 2013).

78 Stewart, 587.

79 Edward M. Shoemaker, "The Immigrant Community of Savannah 1837-1866" (PhD dissertation abstract, Emory University, 1990).

80 Ibid.

81 Stewart, 588.

82 "Emmett Park monument salutes service of the 182 Savannah Marines of Dog Company," *Savannah Morning News*, April 1, 2006, www.savannahnow.com (accessed November 6, 2012).

83 James Barlament, "Salzburgers," www.georgiaencyclopedia.org, November 3, 2006 (accessed February 13, 2013).

84 Georgia Salzburger Society, "Salzburger," http://georgiasalzburgers.com/salzburgers.htm (accessed February 13, 2013).

85 Ibid.

86 Ibid.

87 Lutheran Press, www.lutheranpress.com.

88 Susie Chisholm, www.susiechisholm.com/bio.html (accessed January 19, 2013).

89 Lesley Conn, "Familiar faces spur Haitian furor over Savannah monument," *Savannah Morning News*, October 28, 2009, http:// www.savannahnow.com (accessed October 22, 2012). Photos.

90 James Mastin, Key West Historic Memorial Sculpture Garden, www.keywestsculpturegarden.org (accessed May 9, 2011).

91 Lesley Conn.

92 Ibid.

93 Ibid.

94 Ibid.

95 The German Friendly Society of Savannah History, germanfriendlysociety.com/History (accessed January 12, 2012).

96 Hugh Golson, "The Extraordinary Heritage of German-speaking People Found in Savannah, Georgia," Coastal Heritage Society, www.willkommei-savannah.com (accessed April 3, 2013).

97 Ibid.

98 "The History of Carver State Bank," The Savannah Tribune, June 27, 2012, www.savannahtribune.com (accessed June 19, 2012).

99 Ced Dodler, "Clermont Lee (b. 1914)," www.georgiaencyclopedia.com, April 1, 2005 (accessed May 7, 2012).

100 "Over 300 Years of Old World Craftsmanship,"
     Kenneth Lynch and Sons Inc., www.
     klynchandsons.com, 2011 (accessed October
     10, 2012).

101 Institute of Southern Jewish Life, 2006, www.
     isjl.org (accessed September 26, 2012).

102 Spradley, 71.

103 Mary Landers, "Forgotten Chamber located
     beneath Wright Square," Savannah Morning
     News, July 4, 2012, www.savannahnow.com,
     (accessed July 11, 2012).

104 "First African Baptist Church History," First
     African Baptist Church, http://firstafricanbc.
     com/history.asp, 2011 (accessed March 13,
     2013).

105 Charles Elmore, "Ralph Mark Gilbert Civil
     Rights Museum," www.georgiaencyclopedia.
     com, April 26, 2004 (accessed March 13, 2013).

106 "City of Savannah Fire Department History,"
     Savannah Fire and Emergency, www.
     savannahga.gov (accessed April 11, 2013).

107 Ibid.

108 Charles Gray, "Monument to Honor Long-
     Gone Fire Companies," WTOC, October 11,
     2007, www.wtoc.com (accessed July 20, 2012).

109 International Seamen's House, www.
     seameshouse.org (accessed June 3, 2013).

110 "Police Officers Monument," http://HMdb.org
     (accessed July 2, 2012).

111 Roger M. Williams, "Who's Got Button's
     Bones?" American Heritage Magazine, Vol. 7
     Issue 2, February 1996.

112 Ibid.

113 Ibid.

114 Roland Bainton, Here I Stand, New York:
     Abingdon Cokesbury Press, 1951, 120.

115 Aaron Spencer Fogleman, "Moravians," www.
     georgiaencyclopedia.com, December 10, 2005
     (accessed November 5, 2012).

116 Ibid.

117 Ibid.

118 Kathy W. Ross and Rosemary Stacy, "John
     Wesley and Savannah." The Savannah Images
     Project, www.armstrong.edu/Methodism/
     wesley/html (accessed February 12, 2013).

119 Ibid.

120 Ibid.

121 Ibid.

122 Jane Fishman, "Yamacraw art projects been a
     struggle, but artist keeps the faith," Savannah
     Morning News, May 18, 2001, http://www.
     savannahnow.com (accessed April 13, 2013),

123 "Yamacraw Public Art Project: 'The Mother of
     public art projects' is finally unveiled Saturday
     afternoon," Savannah Morning News, May 13,
     2006, www.savannahnow.com (accessed April
     2013).

124 "Henry McNeal Turner," This Far by Faith
     series, 2003, www.pbs.org (accessed July 7,
     2013).

125 "Henry McNeal Turner: I Claim the Rights
     of a Man," Black Past.org: Remembered and
     Reclaimed, www.blackpast.org (accessed June
     23, 2013).

126 Cain Hope Felder, "Henry McNeal Turner This
     Far by Faith," www.pbs.org, 2003.

127 Fresh Air Home, www.thefreshairhome-tybee.
     org (accessed June 3, 2013).

128 "History," Fresh Air Home: Tybee Beach, www.
     thefreshairhome-tybee.org (accessed May 19,
     2013).

BIBLIOGRAPHY

Bondurant, Emmet. "The Scottish Plymouth Rock." Darien, Georgia. www.home.sprintmail. com/~ejb/Darien.htm (accessed April 7, 2011).

Brandell Studios. http://brandellstudios.com (accessed June 13, 2012).

Busch, John Lawrence. *Steam Coffin: Captain Moses Rogers and The Steamship Savannah Break the Barrier.* Hodos Historia, 2010.

Chisholm. Susie Chisholm. www.susiechisholm.com/bio.html (accessed January 22, 2013).

Congregation Mickve Israel. http://mickveisrael.org (accessed April 4, 2012).

Conlon. Kevin. www.dl.dropboxusercontent. com/w/2154968/website/index.html. Kevin Conlon: Online Portfolio (accessed May 8, 2013).

Cope, Tony. On the Swing Shift: Building Liberty Ships in Savannah, Naval Institute Press, 2009. http://blog.usni.org/2009/11/16/on-the-swing-shift-building-liberty-ships-in-savannah-by-tony-cope (accessed January 13, 2012).

Freeman, Ron. *Savannah: People, Places, and Events.* Tallahassee, FL: Rose Printing Co., 2011.

Gamble, Thomas. *Savannah Monuments.* N.p., n.d.

Georgia Salzburger Society. www.georgiasalzburgers. com (accessed February 13, 2013).

Golway, Terry. *Washington's General: Nathaniel Greene and the Triumph of the American Revolution.* New York: Henry Holt and Company, 2006.

International Seamen's House. www.seamenshouse. org (accessed June 3, 2013).

Jordan, Abigail Hester Williams. *Trials and Tribulations of Building an African-American Monument in Savannah, Georgia; 1991-2002.* Self-published, 2008.

Kammen, Michael. *Digging Up the Dead: A History of Notable American Reburials.* Chicago: University of Chicago Press, 2010.

Lears, Jackson. *Rebirth of a Nation: The Making of Modern America, 1877-1920.* New York: Harper Perennial, 2009.

Lenkiewicz, Antoni. One More Funeral of Kazimierz Pulaski. www.poles.org/lenkiewicz.html (accessed October 11, 2011).

Middlekauff, Robert. *The Glorious Cause: The American Revolution, 1763-1789.* Oxford: Oxford University Press, 2005.

Mills, Cynthia, and Pamela H. Simpson, editors. *Monuments to the Lost Cause: Women, Art and the Landscapes of Southern Memory.* Knoxville: University of Tennessee, 2003.

Piechocinski, Elizabeth Carpenter. *Men of Iron Men of Stone Feet of Clay: A History of Savannah's Gifted Artisans.* Savannah, GA: Oglethorpe Press, 2006.

Rotary International. http://rotary.org/AboutUs/ History (accessed April 19, 2012).

Savannah Morning News. Various. Archives (accessed 2010-2013).

Shoemaker, Edward M. "Strangers and Citizens: The Irish Immigrant Community of Savannah 1837-1861." PhD diss., Emory University, 1990.

Stewart, Dorothy. *The Monuments and Foundations of Savannah: A Report on an Internship for the Savannah Park and Tree Department.* Self-published, 1993.

Thurmond, Michael. *Freedom: Georgia's Antislavery Heritage.* Atlanta: Longstreet Press, 2003.

Underwood, Sandra L. Art in Savannah: *A Guide to the Monuments and Museums Galleries and Other Places.* Atglen, PA: Schiffer Publishing, Ltd., 2007.

United Daughters of the Confederacy. www.hqudc. org (June 2013).

Williams, Roger M. "Who's Got Button's Bones?" American Heritage 17, issue 2 (February 1996).